*The
German
Texans*

The German Texans

Glen E. Lich

The University of Texas
Institute of Texan Cultures
at San Antonio
1996

The German Texans
by Glen E. Lich

Copyright © 1996
The University of Texas Institute of Texan Cultures at San Antonio
801 South Bowie Street, San Antonio, Texas 78205-3296

International Standard Book Number 0-86701-072-X

Revised edition 1996
        (First edition 1981)

This publication was made possible, in part, by grants and gifts from the
following foundations, agencies, and individuals:

        German participants in the Texas Folklife Festival;
        Doc and Gertrude Neuhaus of Mission;
        The Order of the Sons of Hermann;
        Edna Feuge Faust Memorial Trust—
                First National Bank of New Braunfels, Trustee;
        The Store of the Institute of Texan Cultures;
        The Institute of Texan Cultures Associates;
        Wurstfest Association of New Braunfels;
        and the Houston Endowment, Inc.

Printed in the United States of America

C O N T E N T S

P R E F A C E

The German Texans is a scrapbook of favorite personal clippings from the past, a collection of lives, events, pictures, and memories. It is also a view of Texas history through the eyes of some of the most thoughtful and observant members of this ethnic group.

These interesting people tell of their strengths and weaknesses, their anxieties, their frustrations, their humor, and their love of life. They explain how life looked to them, what it meant either at the time or looking back on it later, sometimes arguing among themselves, sometimes in total agreement. The sketches, events, paintings, and recollections are seldom complete on their own, but together they present a whole picture.

From our vantage point, the things these people said may not always accurately reflect life or the conditions of the times. But the German Texans made these judgments, and their own words belong to their self-portrait.

This book attempts to introduce as many aspects of the German-Texan heritage as possible in a small volume conceived for a general readership. The five chapters are impressionistic in their necessarily compressed and selective treatment of large subjects, such as the political, economic, and intellectual climate of a troubled Germany in the early 1800's, or the often difficult assimilation of the German immigrants into mainstream American political and economic life. A chronology at the end of the book includes the Germans in a broader context of central European colonization in Texas, and it places the entire migration in a framework of significant events which have patterned the state's and region's development. The bibliography lists basic English-language works, available in most public libraries or readily attainable through interlibrary loan, and two German-language references to facilitate genealogical research.

The picture essays bring the themes of each chapter together graphically. Their purpose is to evoke feelings about history, feelings that transcend facts, feelings from which the national myths of each age spring.

Glen E. Lich
Cypress Creek
July 1978

"We hurried toward the sinking sun, the magic West beckoning."

*I*n the 19th century, the lure of the Texas frontier attracted outsiders to a land which promised adventure, abundance, and good fortune. Early Texas was a wilderness dream for Americans and Europeans. Some people imagined a new Garden of Eden where disheartened people could make a new start. Others saw Texas as an experiment in democracy, a chance for liberty and prosperity. Still others searched for freedom from the limitations of a worn-out homeland, from the taxes and hopeless debts, even from the law or a troubled past.

Every dream is fed by myths and legends, and the dream of Texas as a great golden land is no exception. One myth started with a young romantic rebel named Karl Anton Postl, who escaped from a European monastery and fled from Germany to the New World under the assumed name of Charles Sealsfield. His novel about Texas life in the 1830's, *The Cabin Book*, became a European bestseller. Texas for Sealsfield was a "boundless sea of green," an unspoiled garden in "God's world immaculate." The land was immeasurably beautiful and rich, inhabited by legendary men, where "nails grew overnight into horseshoes." Sealsfield admitted there was "indeed a lot of rabble in Texas," but he assured his readers that the bones of such Texans would "pave the road into a better tomorrow. Why do we love America?" Sealsfield asked. "Because she makes us love Freedom for the whole human race, and stands for the progress of all civilization." [1]

The view toward a new horizon as envisioned by Caspar David Friedrich

These words were welcome in a politically and economically troubled Europe. Especially in Germany, Texas was quite popular as a wild and fabulous land. A restless generation, growing to maturity between the revolutions of 1830 and 1848, was attracted by the opportunities of this new land. One young girl, Ottilie Fuchs, whose father gave up a good position for the uncertainty and hardships of the frontier, recalled her feelings when she saw the ship: "Well do I remember my apprehensions as we boarded this fearsome crate which was to carry us into the New World. Our former home and happy childhood now lay behind us, soon to be followed by more serious times. Yet we were cheerful. There was no lack of singing, everyone attempting to encourage the other, with probably many a secret tear falling into the waves. We hurried towards the sinking sun, the magic West beckoning, as we wondered what the future held in store." [2]

A philosophy professor, whose political views had landed him in prison, turned his back on a distinguished career and set out for Texas with his family. "I will be a free man in a free earth," Dr. Ernst Kapp exclaimed. [3]

A German officer and nobleman, who had long deliberated whether he should leave what he had earned, was not disappointed by what he found in Texas. Writing back to Germany to encourage his friends, Friedrich W. von Wrede reported, "I have seen a rich, beautiful world filled with resources, full of challenges." He warned his countrymen, though, "Not money, not even the sum of one's wishes and hopes will decide his success in the New World. It takes the energy of men who are determined to reach their goal. I know we shall have hard battles to fight, but whoever will fall in this battle, must fall." Then the old veteran added, "I want to work once more with men willing to fight a new country and conquer." [4]

For tradition-bound German families, abandoning their homeland for the New World was a difficult, irrevocable decision touching on every aspect of their lives. Later in life Ottilie Fuchs Goeth recalled of her father, "It does not require any vast psychological knowledge to understand that our father, Pastor Fuchs, wished to provide greater opportunities for his children, rather than allow them to be stifled, body and soul, through the miserable conditions prevailing in Germany. To understand this, one needs only to visualize the rigid bureaucracy of the 1830's and 1840's when Metternich was in power, to sense the impending storm in the political atmosphere precipitating the Revolution of 1848; to recall the tyrannical suppression of the writings of the 'Young Germany' writers, as well as the then-

Vision of the New World—Gartenlaube *by Hermann Lungkwitz*

3

On Live Oak Creek *by Hermann Lungkwitz*

prevailing oppressive rule of the church. Was Pastor Fuchs to watch his girls at most attain positions as governesses, the boys starving themselves to struggle through a university in order, perhaps too by God's will alone, to earn a scanty living, thus perpetuating the old miseries and wants from generation to generation? Or was it not better to go to found a new home? The choice must have been a difficult one, resolutely faced." [5]

Charles Sealsfield's *The Cabin Book* was followed by a large number of travel books, immigrant guides, poems, and songs about Texas. When the group of Germans headed by Pastor Fuchs was sailing for Texas, Hoffmann von Fallersleben, romantic poet and author of the German anthem, "Deutschland, Deutschland über Alles," wrote farewell lyrics entitled "The Star of Texas" in honor of the occasion. Later he wrote a number of other Texas songs, published them in a small songbook, and sent them to his Texas friends.

Other writers and intellectuals of this restless young generation of the 1840's were also enchanted by the New World. Most of them, except those protected by high birth, lived in political exile, and they sympathized with the search for freedom and opportunity which brought so many of their countrymen to the shores of Texas, as well as to other states, South America, and Mexico. Their view of the Germany which had driven them away was bitter. Writers like Georg Büchner, Heinrich Heine, and Ludwig Börne announced that the only cure for the problems of Germany was to leave them behind. These writers had large followings among the radical "Young Germany" liberals.

Inside Germany, in the midst of distinguished literary and political circles, the same sentiment was expressed by Bettina von Arnim, who was the sister of one famous writer, the widow of another, and a friend of Johann Wolfgang von Goethe, Friedrich von Schiller, and the Grimm brothers. Bettina carried her plea for redress of social grievances directly to the king of Prussia. "Politics," she quoted De Tocqueville, "should be directed to the happiness of the little man." [6] Leading a charmed life, Bettina could attempt what few others dared, but her words in *Dies Buch gehört dem König* did nothing to relieve the suffering of Germany's masses. Those who were disillusioned with the hope of overcoming the problems of the homeland dreamed of a "transatlantic Europe" where they would be free and there was hope again.

Not only ethnic Germans but also other nationalities in Europe then governed by or historically associated with the German monarchies took part in the immigration movement to America. A significant part of this migration was directed toward Texas. In this manner Austrians, Swiss, Tyrolians, Alsatians, Bohemians, Wends, and Poles settled in the valleys of the Brazos, Colorado, Navidad, Guadalupe, and San Antonio Rivers.

Bettina von Arnim

Within the larger context, North America had been a goal of German emigration since before the American Revolution. Waves of Germans had come as early as 1710 to New York, New Jersey, Delaware, Pennsylvania, and Maryland. These were followed after 1735 by Germans who settled in the Carolinas, Georgia, and Louisiana. Throughout the 19th century, hundreds of thousands of Germans entered the northern United States and settled, for the most part, in the cities and farming communities of the Midwest. Germans from the Volga Valley and the Black Sea in Russia also settled in the Midwest, where they introduced a rust-resistant strain of wheat which revolutionized American agriculture. Germans and Swiss brought the wine industry to California, and when grapevine blight wiped out the vineyards, it was Germans who discovered a way to graft European varietal grapes on healthy American rootstock.

After Texas gained its independence from Mexico in 1836 in a struggle that caught the fancy of a host of German and American adventurers, the young republic was pictured as a new utopia in popular German travel literature.

Although the search for religious freedom motivated some Germans in the 1700's, it was seldom an active consideration for the majority of German immigrants who reached Texas in the 1800's. Social and economic improvement, along with political idealism, were the primary goals for these Texas settlers. They responded to the ancient German trait affectionately called *Wanderlust,* a romantic yearning for exotic distant lands. They followed their longing for new opportunities, scientific curiosity, and the desire to escape an overcrowded homeland.

One young wanderer named Max Krueger, who stayed in Texas to become a successful merchant, contended, "I may state here without fear of contradiction that no nation in the wide world is subject to such an intense longing for travel as the German people. And along with this desire for adventure is the urge for work. There is neither doctor nor medicine for this state of mind, and many a poor fellow has had to succumb to it. What is it that causes these sentimental longings? It is the German *soul,*" he concluded with exceedingly great pride, "that something that is denied other races and seldom understood by them." [7]

An adventurous and energetic pioneer, Krueger recalled in his memoir, "I longed to get a glimpse of the Wild West. Like many other boys I had read Cooper's *Leatherstocking Tales* and similar Indian stories which represented their redskinned heroes as brave and chivalrous warriors. Those stories and the romance of a life in the wilder-

6

Aus dem Leben
eines Ansiedlers

ness had an alluring influence upon my fancy, and when I read in the
New Orleans *Deutsche Zeitung* a description of the atrocities perpe-
trated by the Comanches and Apaches on the German settlers, I was
fully determined to start for Texas to brave the dangers of the wild
Texas border life and see for myself what it actually was." [8]

The venerable Pastor Adolphus Fuchs himself had been so
inspired as a young man in Germany by James Fenimore Cooper's
book *The Last of the Mohicans* that he and his boyhood hunting com-
panion "always addressed one another as Hawkeye and Uncas, even in
their correspondence." [9]

While at sea in 1848, young Carl Hilmar Guenther, later in-
fluential in San Antonio, explained in a letter to his parents that he
felt tired of the Old Country and disappointed with the prospects of
his future there. "As soon as I left our own home and made little trips
around the country to acquaint myself with conditions in Germany, I

Ottfried Hans von Meusebach

found that nothing appealed to me. Business and life in general seemed dead. Not until I made my final decision to leave did I ever feel joy or peace." [10]

Young Baron Ottfried Hans von Meusebach, who was to become the farsighted leader of large numbers of German colonists in Texas, admitted in an 1844 letter to Count Castell of the Adelsverein that Texas and the frontier appealed to his scientific curiosity. "For several years," he wrote, "I have been considering going to America to obtain a large enough property to be the basis of nature study and furtherance thereof in those rich fields. I have had my eyes especially on Texas." [11]

Chief among the causes of emigration for the great masses of Germans coming to Texas was the problem of overpopulation in the homeland. In the preface of a book banned by the German police in 1829, Gottfried Duden, a German traveler in the United States, wrote that "most of the evils from which the inhabitants of Europe, and particularly of Germany, suffer arise from overpopulation and are of such a nature that all remedies remain without effect unless a thinning out of the population precedes them." [12]

Some emigrants apparently thought to escape what they foresaw as an imminent catastrophe for Europe by coming to America. Franz Kettner, who settled in Comanche lands northwest of Fredericksburg, expressed this in a letter to Germany. "Much land around here has been bought by people still living in Germany who want a place of refuge to come to during the bad times which will soon come to Germany. All people in America are agreed that there will be a mighty clash in Germany, yes, in all of Europe, in which not even a child will be safe. America will not remain neutral in the coming revolution but will help the republicans. Our country gains strength every year and could show the Old World who is boss." [13]

By the early 1840's, several thousand Germans had survived the eight- to twelve-week voyages across the Atlantic to new homes in the Republic of Texas. They came predominantly from provinces in northern Germany and concentrated in Austin, Colorado, Fayette, Washington, DeWitt, and Victoria Counties.

German interest in Texas entered a new phase in 1842, when an assembly of five sovereign princes and 16 noblemen convened at Biebrich on the Rhine near Mainz and formed a society to promote German colonization in Texas. This poorly organized, uninformed, badly underfinanced organization is best known as the Adelsverein.

The first colonists sponsored by the Adelsverein landed at Galveston and then sailed to Indianola in 1844. The records of the German Immigration Company in the Texas General Land Office in Austin indicate that most of these settlers were from the provinces of western and northwestern Germany. Despite the great misery of the first two years, the Adelsverein brought nearly 7,400 German immigrants to Texas between 1844 and 1847. As the massive migration gained momentum from then until 1860, about 20,000 more Germans moved to Texas.

The Adelsverein Germans established New Braunfels, Fredericksburg, and several villages on the Llano River. Smaller farming communities in Bexar, Guadalupe, Comal, Blanco, Gillespie, Mason, Kendall, and Kerr Counties grew from these settlements. In the Hill Country today, more than in any other place in Texas, this European culture from the Adelsverein colonists has lingered to the end of the 20th century.

A farm village in the early 1800's . . .
Jobs in the German cities and countryside were scarce, and laborers were poorly paid. Taxes were often oppressive, and few people had more money than was required to buy necessities. The real problems throughout Germany were widespread poverty and a population too large to be supported adequately by the resources of the land, yet prices paid to farmers for their produce were quite low, and a great deal of bartering went on in the town because of the scarcity of money. Ministers and schoolteachers were sometimes paid "in kind" for their services, which meant that their salaries were exchanges of food, clothing, and lodging rather than money.

The poverty was terribly oppressive. Young men, unless they inherited their fathers' business or land, had no place to go. By law most farms could not be divided, so only one child in a family inherited a secure income. Girls had one choice—marriage, and it was hard to start a new family without a house to live in.

One town chronicle reports that for years no one could afford sugar. During these years a special treat for children, the chronicle continues, was the "oven cake," which mothers made by splitting open a potato and roasting it atop the wood stove in the kitchen, then spreading it with bacon drippings.

J.B.C. Corot

LUDWIG BÖRNE

*A*ccording to a friend in 1827, the German "republican" journalist Ludwig Börne was "a peaceful man of small stature, very delicate but not sickly, a small head with thinning black hair, just a touch of red in the cheeks, jovial light brown eyes, with kindness and human warmth in his face and in every gesture, a friendly tone in his voice."

Born in 1786 in Frankfurt am Main as Löw Baruch, he spent his childhood in the degrading ghetto existence of an Orthodox Jew of that city. Börne traveled to Paris immediately after the July 1830 revolution and remained in France until his death in 1837.

He was the first German journalist whose writings usually criticized the conservative political order in Germany. He attacked reactionary attitudes and supported popular freedom movements in his fatherland. His criticism was at times witty, at times satirical.

Börne devoted all of his efforts to promoting a liberalism in Germany after the French example. "He was a patriot from his crown to his smallest toe," said his one-time friend and later enemy Heinrich Heine. Börne's *Letters from Paris* (1832-1834), marked by a passionate and moving love of country, strongly influenced a small but radical group of writers who called themselves "Young Germany."

Of freedom and life only he is deserving
    Who every day must conquer them anew.
America! You are more fortunate
    Than this old world . . .
Aye! such a throng I fain would see
    Stand on a free earth, among a people free.

J.W. v. Goethe

"The Battle Song of San Jacinto" by Hoffman von Fallersleben,
translated into English by Adolphus Fuchs

HOPE

    Men sing and dream of better days and hunt for golden treasure. Countries rise and countries fall, but people search on for richer lives.

    Hope brings man into the world and clothes the joyful child. The youth pursues its gentle call, but it survives the old man's grave. . . .

    It is no empty, vague delusion in the mind of fools; the heart proclaims that we are born for better worlds. And what the inner spirit speaks is not lost on the soul that seeks.

Friedrich von Schiller

THE STAR OF TEXAS

A farewell poem for our dear Pastor Fuchs
(The melody is that of "Nach Seville.")

On to Texas, on to Texas,
    Where the star in blue field
Prophesies a new world,
    And makes every heart burn
For right and freedom and for truth—
    This is where my heart longs to go.
On to Texas, on to Texas,
    Where the curse of tradition
And the old blind faith
    In the face of pure human love
Is finally turned to ashes and dust—
    This is where my heart longs to go.
On to Texas, on to Texas,
    Where the plow becomes the sign
Of reconciliation and uprising,
    So that mankind can celebrate again
Their May Day of revival—
    This is where my heart longs to go.
On to Texas, on to Texas,
    Golden star, you are the messenger
Of our new, better lives:
    Since what free hearts hope,
They never hope in vain.
    Welcome to you, golden star!

August Hoffmann von Fallersleben

13

MEUSEBACH AND THE BERLIN CIRCLE
Tranquility in a Troubled Time

*B*aron Ottfried Hans von Meusebach was educated for a career befitting the son of an ancient family. As a boy he first studied mining and natural sciences, then law, government, economics, and banking. He read five languages and spoke English quite fluently.

When his father, a high justice, moved his family from Meusebach's boyhood home on the Rhine to Berlin, young Meusebach was introduced into the elegant society of the Prussian capital. He especially impressed the charming Bettina von Arnim, who was struck by the young man's inquisitive and idealistic mind. He was a likeable fellow and shared Bettina's devotion for the great poet Johann Wolfgang von Goethe.

Through Bettina von Arnim and others, Meusebach became acquainted with some of Germany's greatest writers and intellectuals. This "Berlin Circle" included General von Clausewitz (the most important modern military tactician), the Humboldt brothers (one a minister of state and founder of the new Berlin University, the other a scientist and explorer), the Grimm brothers (philologists who helped establish the modern study of folklore with their collections of German fairy tales), the critic Varnhagen von Ense (whose nephew came to Texas), and August Hoffmann von Fallersleben (who wrote the Texas songs).

Their political views were far ahead of their time in conservative Prussia. Here Meusebach heard the first echoes of utopian socialistic experiments like Brook Farm in America. He also shared the concern of the Berlin Circle that the tyranny of Prince Metternich's police state had closed the door on liberalism and nationalism, the twin daughters of the French Revolution.

As a lawyer and later as mayor of a small Prussian town, Meusebach worked for national unity and political freedom, but he could accomplish little since these reforms were outlawed by the government. Still he was inspired by an idea from the philosopher Fichte that "every man must, in the most literal sense, carve out his own destiny." Like many younger people, Meusebach was disheartened by the conditions he saw in his homeland, and although he hated to think of leaving Germany, he knew he had no real future there. He discussed the matter of leaving with his family. His father warned that life would not be easy. His mother only advised, "Finish what you begin, son."

The novelist Sealsfield's picture of Texas as a savage and exotic land haunted Meusebach's mind, and he brought the matter up with Bettina and others of the Berlin Circle, where considerable New World idealism prevailed as a result of Baron Alexander von Humboldt's explorations and the journeys of Prince Maximilian von Wied and Duke Paul of Württemberg.

On the night that he spoke with the group about going to America, Bettina had brought along a young friend, a strikingly beautiful girl named Elisabethe von Hardenberg. She listened attentively to the young man's visions of the New World and its opportunities.

A warm friendship began between them that night, and they saw much of each other in the following months. Elisabethe was also fascinated by the New World and thought that she could be happy there. Eventually Meusebach made his decision to sail for Texas but not until he and Elisabethe had promised each other to marry upon his return. Then they would return together to the home he would prepare for her in Texas.

Drawing by Elisabethe von Hardenberg, a fantasy influenced by Charles Sealsfield

Behr adapted to the new land without great difficulty. His log and half-timber, or Fachwerk, *home on the Guadalupe near Sisterdale was the stopping place of travelers Duke Paul of Württemberg and Frederick Law Olmsted. It contained a harpsichord, a post office, and Behr's own office as justice of the peace.*

Ottomar von Behr was the son of the prime minister of Anhalt-Köthen and an acquaintance of Alexander von Humboldt and Bettina von Arnim.

OTTOMAR VON BEHR

*O*ne pioneer of the Hill Country, Ottomar von Behr, was seriously concerned with the problems facing German farmers in a rugged terrain with thoroughly unpredictable weather unlike anything in Germany. The scholarly Behr wrote a very practical book, *Good Advice for Immigrants*, on farming and ranching in Texas, with particular emphasis on the advantages of sheep raising.

THE ADELSVEREIN
An Essay in Pictures

*T*he eyes of all Germany, no, the eyes of all Europe are fixed on us and our undertaking; German princes, counts, and noblemen stand at the head and no doubt can remember the historical glory of their ancestors and bring new crowns to old glory while they at the same time are ensuring immeasurable riches for their children and grandchildren.

Prince Carl of Solms-Braunfels

No sooner had a favorable report come back from Texas in 1843 than the Adelsverein determined upon a grand colonization scheme. The next year the members, now having grown to 24 rulers and nobles, incorporated as a stock company, and "a resolution was adopted that speculation and political projects were not contemplated and that the society, out of purely philanthropical reasons, would devote itself to the support and direction of German emigration to Texas." [14] The following four objectives were formulated:

to improve the lot of the working class who are without
employment, thus controlling their increasing poverty;
to unite the emigrants by giving them protection
through this Association in order to ease their burden by
mutual assistance;
to maintain contacts between Germany and the emigrants, and to develop maritime trade by establishing
business connections;
to find a market for German crafts in these settlements,
and to provide a market in Germany for the products of
these colonies. [15]

With this, the leaders considered the major part of the undertaking
completed. All that remained, they naively thought, was getting the
emigrants together in Antwerp or Bremen, provisioning, transport-
ing, and lodging them, and finding a suitable place for settlement. It
was decided that the 4,000-acre Nassau Farm purchased for this purpose in Fayette County was too close to existing American towns for
the Germans to be able to preserve their identity. Furthermore, the
Adelsverein's 3,000,000-acre holding, the so-called "Fisher-Miller
Grant" which lay between the Llano and Colorado Rivers in West
Texas, was largely unsuited to farming and wholly occupied by hostile
Indians. Immediately upon his arrival in Texas, Prince Solms negotiated the purchase of a tract of land on the Guadalupe River for the
first German settlement under the auspices of the Adelsverein.

Abschied der Auswanderer —The Emigrant's Farewell
Pioneer Memorial Museum, Fredericksburg

*Carl, Prince of Solms,
Lord of Braunfels, Grafenstein,
Münzenberg, Wildenfels, and
Sonnenwalde, Commissioner-
General of the Society for the
Protection of German
Immigrants in Texas,
the Adelsverein*

*Duke Adolph of Nassau,
Protector of the Adelsverein*

*Braunfels Castle
on the Lahn River
in Germany*

Prince Frederick of Prussia

The ancient way of life yielded only slowly to the forces of time. For the peasant whose livelihood sprang from the earth, the bonds that held these men to their homeland were not simple, personal ones. The ties were deeper, more intimate. The peasant was part of a community, and the community was held to the land as a whole. Always the start was the village. This was the fixed point by which he knew his relationship with all humanity.

Oscar Handlin

The contractual terms between the noblemen and the colonists were carefully stipulated in written documents bearing the Adelsverein seal with the Lone Star and clutch of arrows. Upon payment of fees, each emigrant was promised a specified number of acres under the conditions that he live on the land for three years, fence and cultivate 15 acres of land, build a dwelling on his property, and submit in his conduct to the rules of the Society and the laws of the land.

Immigration contract from the General Land Office, Austin

Prince Solms's coat of arms

THE VOYAGE
As a young girl remembered it . . .

Our journey in the fall of the year was at the worst imagin-
able time to sail. The food was wretched, the water barely
drinkable, and we were seasick throughout most of the
voyage. It was particularly rough in the North Sea, with its choppy
green waves.

Ottilie Fuchs Goeth, 1840's

And as recalled by a wealthy matron—

*W*e have bid Bremen farewell since yesterday and spent our first night on the ship. As soon as all packages are loaded and arranged and the wind is somewhat more favorable, we shall be on our way. The cabin is large, and alongside are the rooms, which can be locked, each of which sleeps four persons, two below and two above. The bunks are sufficiently wide and long; only the height is lacking, but we will get used to that. Above our deck is a very elegant cabin which costs no more and has many advantages. Unfortunately, it was taken. However, we have the right to go there. Our cabin holds 32. There are many young and very noble-appearing young men on board. And there is Dr. Ernst Kapp and his family and, most interesting of all, the Austrian Deputy with wife and child. The woman sweeps the stairs with her yellow dress and mantilla. Also we have the Frankfurt Deputy, Hertzberg.

A little bell summoned us to the deck. The captain, standing in front of a festively decorated pulpit, read a suitable song out of a Reformed Church hymnal and then read with a loud strong voice an uplifting poem entitled "The Storm" from the *Ocean Temple*. The poem described the circumstances of the emigrants, from the weak to the strong man, the dangers of the ocean voyage, the storm and the rescue, the new and often sad conditions of the new home. It was so affecting that eyes were filled while all about us was the surging ocean, the swaying ship, and the poorly clad folks from the middle deck who sat at the captain's feet with devout faces paled by seasickness.

Amanda Fallier von Rosenberg
aboard the *Franziska,* 1840's

RATIONS AT SEA

Sunday
  Plum soup
  ½ lb. beef
  Meal pudding

Monday
  Pea soup
  ½ lb. pork
  Thick rice with syrup

Tuesday
  Barley soup
  ½ lb. beef
  Lentils or beans

Wednesday
  Navy bean soup
  ½ lb. beef
  Sauerkraut or green beans

Thursday
  Plum soup
  ½ lb. beef
  Meal pudding

Friday
  Pea soup
  ½ lb. pork
  Sauerkraut or green beans

Saturday
  Green pea soup
  ½ lb. beef
  Lentils or beans

Weekly rations for each adult
  4 oz. coffee
  2 oz. tea
  8 oz. sugar
  16 oz. butter
  5 lb. bread
  ¼ bottle wine

Further, for each adult
  1½ hogshead drinking water
    for voyage to Texas
  30-40 lbs. potatoes,
    according to season
  Salt, mustard, pepper,
    vinegar, medicines

Sophienburg Museum

24

One of my relatives who had gone to Texas in the forties with the Adelsverein had come back on a visit. . . . He told many enthusiastic stories about his new home. I was thrilled when I listened to him describing the charms of that recently opened paradise, the eternally blue sky, the radiant sun above the great uncultivated, uninhabited land, tempting tropical fruits, Indians and wild animals, too, to break the monotony of existence, and above all else, golden freedom. Texas became the land of my dreams.

Emma Murck Altgelt

"I will be a free man in a free earth."

*H*opeless conditions on the Continent turned the minds of many Germans to the dream of building a model homeland in the New World. This ideal of a "New Germany" in America united people from all walks of life. Doctors, teachers, ministers, scientists, merchants, artisans, farmers, students, and soldiers defied laws prohibiting their departure. Professionals gave up promising careers, while farmers sold out at losses or even forfeited their lands, and women and children sacrificed their established homes for hardships and uncertain futures.

They were a courageous lot, and many lost their lives. Most were completely unprepared for the experiences they encountered, and some failed dismally. But all shared the feeling that the promise of success growing from their hard work far outweighed their former security. Professor Ernst Kapp, accustomed to the genteel life of the cities, expressed what many felt.

"I depart voluntarily from my teaching position. I leave Germany, exchanging comfort for toil, the familiar pen for the unfamiliar spade, but I will be a free man in a free earth."

Texas was an adventure, the brink of the unknown, and life in the New World was an abrupt change, laden with hardship and danger. The undertaking was especially difficult for immigrants who tried it alone. Going into a strange land encouraged relatives and friends to stay together for protection and assurance.

Sometimes, though, a particularly adventurous individual went ahead to scout out the best location for settlement. These "trailblazers" then sent home instructions for those who waited to follow. With ties strengthened by kinship, association, and letters, neighbors from villages in Germany often settled together in the strange new homeland.

Initially these Germans settled in small farm villages. As the population increased and the towns grew, farmers and ranchers moved across a vast expanse of land, carrying civilization farther and farther westward.

Early Settlers

The arrival in 1831 of Friedrich Ernst and Charles Fordtran marked the real beginning of German colonization in Texas. Ernst, former head gardener and bookkeeper for the Duke of Oldenburg, and Fordtran, a tanner from Westphalia, joined forces in New York in their search for a new home. Friedrich Ernst brought his large family with him; Fordtran was single. They took passage to New Orleans with the intention of going up the Mississippi to Missouri, where large numbers of Germans were settling.

In New Orleans, however, they learned that every settler who came to Texas with his family would receive a league of land from the Mexican government. Missouri was forgotten, and the small group secured transportation to the Texas coast. Ernst's daughter, later Caroline von Hinüber, said of her first impression, "We landed at Harrisburg, which consisted of about five or six log houses, a sawmill, and a store or two. We remained five weeks, while Fordtran went ahead of us." [16]

"From Harrisburg," her mother wrote, "we continued by oxcart to the town of San Felipe de Austin, located fifty miles to the west. The town had 300 to 400 inhabitants. Here we now sat on the edge of all civilization, because just westerly the Indians lived, and no white man had ever crossed the Mill Creek. My husband undertook an inspection from here in order to select some land, and thus he came to the fords of the creek where Industry is now located. Since the romantic location with its beautiful waters and woods pleased my husband, he had one league of land surveyed by the Mexican commissioner." [17]

To the Germans, the earlier Spanish settlements to the west were unknown and were no support for their efforts. They indeed felt they were the first settlers.

Friedrich Ernst, like many who followed, was ill-prepared for pioneering. He did not know how to build a cabin, hated guns, and had brought none of the necessary equipment for clothing his family on the frontier. Still, he had an unbounded love for his new country, and he poured out his feelings in an eloquent letter to a friend in Oldenburg, urging him to come to Texas at once. The man turned the letter over to a local newspaper, and it was widely published. Ernst's contagious enthusiasm spread through the German states, starting the first steady stream of German migration to Texas. Ernst assured fellow immigrants, "I have a stopping place on my estate for my countrymen until they have selected a league of land. Colonel Austin has recently promised to take care that German arrivals be settled immediately." [18]

Many knew Texas only through Friedrich Ernst's letter. According to an account written in 1876 by Robert Justus Kleberg Sr., father of prominent South Texas rancher Robert J. Kleberg Jr., whose descendants today own the King Ranch, the Ernst letter painted an irresistibly beautiful landscape, "with enchanting scenery and delightful climate similar to that of Italy, the most fruitful soil and republican government, with unbounded personal and political liberty, free from so many disadvantages and evils of old countries." [19] Despite these glowing advantages, the new participants had difficulty in making a fresh start. "Most of them," Friedrich Ernst's daughter observed, "managed very badly at first, using all their money before they had learned to accommodate themselves to their new surroundings." [20]

Rosa von Roeder Kleberg, a young bride when she came, confessed that circumstances were very different from their expectations. "My brothers had pictured pioneer life as one of hunting and fishing, of freedom from the restraints of Prussian society; and it was hard for them to settle down to the drudgery and toil of splitting rails and cultivating the field, work which was entirely new to them."

Rosa Kleberg's father was Ludwig Sigismund Anton von Roeder, who, with his family, left Marienmünster, their feudal estate, to follow the call of Ernst's letter. The father at first carried on a butcher's trade in Harrisburg while the von Roeder sisters learned to sew and make clothing for sale. "We were all unused to that kind of work," Rosa Kleberg later stated, "but we felt that we must save our money; and, when required by necessity, one learns to do what one has never done before. We had our pleasures, though. Our piano had been damaged; but we played on it anyway, and the young people danced to the music." [21]

The settlement of Ernst and Fordtran in Austin County grew into a small German village. Named "Industry" by neighboring Anglo-Americans, who were amazed at the speed with which the German "greenhorns" caught on, the town became a favorite stopping place for immigrants on their way from landings on the Texas coast to their new homesites in the interior. Although Industry was actually the first German settlement in Texas, its official founding dates from 1838 when Ernst laid out the town. By then three other German settlements were in existence. Biegel in Fayette County was established in 1832. Biegel's Settlement, as it was also known, was a cosmopolitan gathering of German- and French-speaking settlers from the French province of Lorraine, the German-speaking cantons of Switzerland, Prussia, Poland, Denmark, and the Rhine Valley. The land, settled in 1834 by Robert Kleberg and the von Roeders was named Cat Spring because one of the von Roeder boys supposedly shot a wildcat there. About three years later, a small group of colonists founded Frelsburg in adjoining Colorado County.

From the coming of Ernst and Fordtran in 1831 to the beginning of organized immigration in 1844, many Germans came to Texas, singly or in small groups. They settled generally at Galveston or Houston or in the fertile valleys between the Brazos and

Charles Fordtran

Colorado Rivers where Ernst had established a foothold. Only 218 Germans were reported in Texas in 1836. Their numbers swelled into the thousands, however, during the 1840's.

The Adelsverein Settlements

In 1842, ten years after Ernst and Fordtran built their first homes near Austin's colony, the Adelsverein sent Prince Leiningen and Count Boos Waldeck to Texas to seek grants for extensive German settlement. Prince Carl of Solms-Braunfels arrived in Galveston the next summer to prepare for the first shiploads of immigrants that winter. He bought a tract on Matagorda Bay to use as a landing place from which the new arrivals could be supplied and organized for their journey into the interior, then negotiated the purchase of lands on the Guadalupe River for a permanent settlement.

Three shiploads of Germans arrived at Galveston in December 1844 and proceeded down the coast to the new port which Prince Carl named Carlshafen, "Carl's Harbor," later known as Indianola on Matagorda Bay. A warehouse and other facilities were erected, but there were no living accommodations for these hundreds of immigrants, weary and sick from their long voyage. Although forced to camp temporarily on the open beach in wet winter weather, these first immigrants fared comparatively well. After a brief stay at Carlshafen, they traveled in wagons and oxcarts to the land Prince Solms had secured for their settlement. On Good Friday,

The houses and businesses of Galveston looked to Europeans like a town of fragile paper toys.

The port of Indianola grew to become an important military depot and export center, then was wrecked by two hurricanes in 1875 and 1886 and became a ghost town.

March 21, 1845, the prince led the first wagon train to this verdant woodland on the border of the swift-running Comal River and established a town, naming it after his ancestral estate of Braunfels on the Lahn River.

New Braunfels, the first colonial German village in Texas, changed quickly from a temporary settlement into a comfortable Old World town on the Texas frontier. In 1846 hospital sheds were built for those who were ill. Teams of men worked together on their own homes, a town church, and a fortress, and then laid out the streets. The following winter, when the second wave of colonists landed on the coast, conditions were altogether different. Funds from Germany for the settlement were depleted because the German nobles had vastly underestimated expenses. Prince Solms had run up large debts in Texas and Louisiana of which he had kept no record. Furthermore, hostilities had broken out between the United States and Mexico, and the teamsters who had previously contracted to transport the new arrivals inland were conscripted to haul weapons and munitions for the army from the Texas coast to Mexico.

Stranded at Carlshafen in miserable shacks and dugouts, approximately a thousand people died, and hundreds more succumbed on the way inland. A daughter of Pastor Louis Cachand Ervendberg, first pastor of the New Braunfels settlement, recounted her parents' description of the misery of this second immigrant trip in 1846.

"They were on the road for a long time, and most of the people had some kind of fever or scurvy from poor food. Some had died in Indianola or were left behind too ill to travel; there were a lot who never lived to reach New Braunfels. It rained all the time, and that made it hard with the oxcarts sticking in the mud and the poor colonists, people who were used to a comfortable life back in Germany, wet and miserable. Then, when they were close enough to see the nice place Prince Solms had ready, there was another big disappointment. The Guadalupe River was so high it could not be crossed, and they had to camp at the old ford. I don't know how long they waited for the river to go down, but several more died there and were buried nearby."

"Provisions were scarce," she continued. "We had plenty of fish from the river, but not much meat. Ammunition was too hard to get. Milk and butter, beef and hog meat all came in due time, as did sweet potatoes and a few vegetables but no Irish potatoes for ever so long. We were hungry for fruit and had to be warned by our doctor against eating the fruit of the cactus. Parched barley and dried sweet potatoes were used when coffee gave out, and the men smoked all kinds of weeds when they couldn't get tobacco. Everything we could not raise for ourselves had to be hauled to us overland. Bales of unbleached cotton cloth had to come . . . from Mexico, and we had to dye it ourselves." [22]

Despite disease and death, New Braunfels grew steadily. Along with hard-working farmers and craftsmen who made up the majority of the Adelsverein immigrants, the arrivals included minor nobles, gentry, and many highly educated intellectuals. When paleontologist and geologist Dr. Ferdinand Roemer, sent by the Berlin Academy, first viewed the fledgling town in 1846, he predicted that the tree-filled market square would be large enough to accommodate a city of 12,000 inhabitants and foresaw that the town's fortunate location would ensure success and steady growth.

Ida Kapp observed that, in 1850, "New Braunfels presented a pitiable impression with its little slab houses along the dirt side streets which during rains became bottomless. There were, however, three bakeries, other artisans, and many stores." Accustomed to fashionable German city life, Mrs. Kapp found the transition to the frontier settlement somewhat abrupt but admitted, "I envy all the young people of 17 and 18 years of age who come here. Even if they come with little or no cash, I firmly believe they can become independent within five to six years if they manage well." [23]

A third eyewitness of the town's growth, a Northerner on a horseback journey through the South in 1857, just 12 years after the founding of New Braunfels, praised the little city because of its fine

Old Lutheran Church in New Braunfels

food. Frederick Law Olmsted, America's great landscape architect, described his dinner on his first night in New Braunfels: "An excellent soup is set before us, and in succession there follow two courses of meat, neither of them pork and neither of them fried, two dishes of vegetables, salad, compote of peaches, coffee with milk, wheat bread from the loaf, and beautiful, sweet butter—not only such butter as I have never tasted south of the Potomac before, but such as I have been told a hundred times it was impossible to make in a southern climate. What is the secret? I suppose it is extreme cleanliness, and careful and thorough working." [24]

In 1845 Prince Solms was replaced as Commissioner General of the Adelsverein by Baron Ottfried Hans von Meusebach, a visionary but practical leader who recognized that the future welfare of the settlers depended upon their becoming "Americans." He encouraged the Germans to spread out into the fertile valleys of the Hill Country; within a year, five new colonies were established in a network of small outposts stretching 150 miles northwest from New Braunfels into the previously unsettled lands of the Comanches.

Meusebach was a perfect leader—intelligent, learned, and sagacious. He found the administrative affairs of the colony in a deplorable condition. Settlers were disgruntled, poorly provisioned, and inadequately housed, and more boatloads were on their way from Germany. Working with great haste, Meusebach was able to straighten out the tangled finances of the colony and reestablish the Adelsverein's credit in Texas. He then bought 10,000 acres on credit on the Pedernales River 80 miles northwest of New Braunfels.

The paleontologist Ferdinand Roemer witnessed the founding of the new colony, named "Friedrichsburg," or "Fredericksburg," in honor of Prince Frederick of Prussia. The departure of colonists to Fredericksburg finally took place on April 23, 1846. The train consisted of 16 wagons, drawn by two or three yoke of oxen, and 180 persons, including the mounted convoy which accompanied the expedition for their protection. The departure of this company proved of general interest also, for it signaled the spread of "civilization" into the northwest Hill Country of Texas. Up to this time, the area was sparsely and exclusively inhabited by roving bands of Indians; whereas the Anglo-American had otherwise been the first to advance into the western wilderness, here the German took on this role.

Although life both in Fredericksburg and in New Braunfels was exceedingly primitive during the first years, one woman in Fredericksburg exclaimed that "it was a great delight to get away from the miserable conditions, the lonesomeness, and the destitution that had surrounded the Germans in Indianola." [25]

John O. Meusebach

In the early days Fredericksburg, the second colony of the Adelsverein, enjoyed a pleasant location but was vulnerable to Indian attack from the surrounding hills.

To secure additional land for his settlers, Meusebach rode into the Indian hunting grounds with a small party. After making peace with the less-warlike Wacos, they continued farther north to deal with the fierce Comanches. According to Dr. Roemer, "When they were still several miles from the valley of the San Saba, a deputation of Comanche Indians met them and inquired the purpose of their coming. Later, on entering the valley itself, a royal reception was accorded them by the Indians. About two hundred dressed in festive attire had arranged themselves on a hill in military formation. After Herr von Meusebach had ridden toward them and by emptying his rifle had given proof of his confidence in them, mutual greetings were exchanged, and a number of presents were distributed among the chiefs."

"The negotiations began after the peace pipe, from which each one took two or three puffs, had made the rounds twice. Herr von Meusebach told the chiefs the following: He had come with his people on the peace path to view the land and to greet them as friends. They would also be received as friends when visiting the cities of his people. He now desired to go up the river to see the old Spanish fort. Upon his return from there, he desired to have a council with the principal chiefs . . . to tell them of his further intentions.

36

"One of the chiefs replied with great dignity as follows: The hearts of his people had been alarmed when they had seen so many strange people, who had not previously announced their coming and whose intention they did not know. But now, since they were assured that they had come as friends and had declared the purpose of their coming, all was well.

"The second meeting with the chiefs took place toward noon. The negotiations proceeded in the manner described previously. After discussing the matter thoroughly, which is characteristic of the mistrustful and cautious nature of the Indians, the proposals made by Herr von Meusebach on the previous day were accepted. The council ended by mutually embracing each other, whereby the Comanches tried to show the degree of their friendship by the strength of their embrace. They were then served a meal of venison and rice which Herr von Meusebach had had prepared for them." [26]

On March 2, 1847, the Comanche chiefs signed a treaty which opened more than 3,000,000 acres of the Fisher-Miller Grant beyond the San Saba River for German colonization and exploration. After the treaty was signed, Meusebach encouraged German families to settle the Hill Country as farmers and ranchers, then turned his attention to another important matter. He had taken the citizenship of Texas immediately upon his arrival (when he also relinquished his hereditary titles and changed his name), and now he assisted the swarm of newcomers in becoming citizens of their adopted land.

Petitions were circulated for the organization of new counties around the German settlements. In 1846 the state legislature created Comal County with New Braunfels as county seat. Fredericksburg became the county seat of Gillespie County in 1848. Two years later Meusebach was elected from these German counties to the state senate. Until the Civil War, he held a number of state appointments regulating headrights, surveys, immigration, public education (the Germans favoring compulsory attendance at nonsectarian schools), and state affairs.

Even during the early years, when he was impeded on every hand by the tottering Adelsverein and its awkward plan of colonization, as well as by the Mexican War, which disrupted domestic transportation, Meusebach's letters attest to his conviction that "German knowledge at the side of American freedom" [27] was creating a haven in the New World.

By 1850 Fredericksburg was slowly approaching a population of 2,000, mostly Germans. Life changed as periods of famine were overcome, and the settlers turned to the pleasant side of life, such as fandangos. "At times the fandangos ended in quarreling," confessed Dr. William Hermes, who treated the victims. "At the beginning of a quarrel, two parties usually were formed: the North Germans were called Hanoverians, and the South Germans, Nassauers, for the two states from which the majority of the Fredericksburg colonists emigrated." [28]

According to most people, however, the difficulties of life in Fredericksburg were a fair price to pay. Writing from the four-year-old settlement, Peter Birk enthusiastically advised his friends in the homeland, "Leave Germany and come here where you can live happily and contentedly. If you work only half as much as in Germany, you can live without troubles. In every sense of the word, we are free. The Indians do us no harm; on the contrary, they bring us meat and horses to buy. We still live so remote from other people that we are lonely, but we have dances, churches, and schools. Buy an old horse to hitch to your wagon, drive it to Bremen, sell your horse, disassemble your wagon to take to America. For the boat trip take a few bottles of syrup and vinegar. Mixed with water this is a very refreshing drink. Bring your rifle. Do not let anyone persuade you to go to any other place than Fredericksburg." [29]

Ten years after the founding of Fredericksburg, the area did suffer a drought so severe that it may have caused settlers like Birk to regret their bright optimism. For a while the outlook was very bleak, and some seriously considered abandoning the settlement. One colonist with a university background in science discovered a clue in nature which gave others some hope. Jacob Kuechler, a Fredericksburg settler of later significance, noted in the tree rings of an old oak that short periods of drought alternated in cycles with longer periods of adequate rainfall. His prediction was right; the lean years were indeed followed by years of plenty.

When the weather improved, prosperity returned, and the settlers again set out to make the good life. One young man found only a few basics lacking. "If you can," he wrote a friend in Germany, "send some wine and with it a pretty woman, young and beautiful. She does not have to have much money, only enough for the trip over here. I also expect that she will be musically inclined and will bring a piano. I require more in a prospective wife now. Then the wine could also be used at the wedding. First, however," he added for safety, "I want a portrait of the one you have chosen for me." [30]

After the establishment of Fredericksburg and the conclusion of the Comanche Treaty, the colonization of the Adelsverein

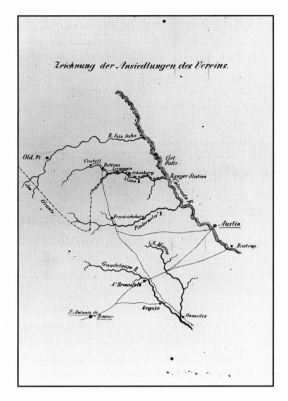

Colonization
of the Adelsverein

entered its last phase. Meusebach made initial preparations in 1847 for a network of new settlements beyond the Llano River. Three of these small villages—Leiningen, Meerholz, and Schönburg—were subsequently abandoned for various reasons. The fourth, Castell, survived but only with prolonged support and provisions from the settlers at Fredericksburg. During the first year, while the colony got under way, tasks were divided for mutual support. "One group of seven felled trees; another built houses; a third group built fences; the fourth did ploughing; and two men watched the cattle. One out of each seven cooked for the group. Each Sunday morning an assembly took place for discussion of alternating tasks amongst the groups." [31] Yet, despite such careful regimentation of manpower, Castell never grew to any extent. By 1850 the village had declined to only seven families and five bachelors for a total population of 32.

Bettina, unique among these Llano settlements, was named for Bettina von Arnim. This visionary undertaking began when Prince Solms addressed members of a fraternity of communistic

39

freethinkers in Germany, telling them "that there was no demand in the Old Country for all the professional men whom universities were turning out, and they must find a new and developing country where their services would be in demand." [32]

Known as "the Forty" from the size of their membership, the fraternity had chapters at Darmstadt, Giessen, and Heidelberg.

In Texas the members hoped to realize their dream of a communistic utopia. The students "had no regular scheme of government," so far as Louis Reinhardt, one member, recalled. "In fact, being communistic, the association would not brook the tyranny of a ruler." Instead there were guiding spirits by common consent, he continued. "Being the youngest of the company—I was thirteen— I was, of course, rarely consulted." [33]

No doubt remained after Prince Solms's meeting with them that the place to seek their ideal community was Texas—"a land of milk and honey, of perennial flowers, of crystal streams, rich and fruitful beyond measure, where roamed myriads of deer and buffalo while the primeval forests abounded in wild fowl of every kind."

For all their youthful dreams of starting a communistic city, the Forty did not have at their command all the practical skills needed to clear virgin land for settlement. Their training was, nonetheless, quite diversified: two physicians, one engineer, two architects, seven lawyers, five foresters, two mechanics, two carpenters, one butcher, one blacksmith, one lieutenant of artillery, one ship carpenter, one brewer, one miller, one hosteler, one theologian, one maker of musical instruments, an agriculturist, and a botanist. Few spoke English, and only a few had ever earned their own living.

Their lack of frontier experience left them little chance of success in Texas. In less than a year, the Bettina experiment "went to pieces like a bubble." Some of the members spent their days hunting in the river bottom, and others did nothing but engage in philosophical debates, while the rest quibbled about work details. "Most of the professional men wanted to do the directing and ordering," recalled the 13-year-old botanist Reinhardt, "while the mechanics and laborers were to carry out their plans. Of course, the latter failed to see the justice of their ruling, so no one did anything." The remaining members of the Forty scattered to San Antonio, New Braunfels, and Austin, where they eventually settled back into the occupations for which they had been trained.

With the decline of Bettina, the work of the Adelsverein also ground to a halt. The organization was bankrupt, and also, after the annexation of Texas, most of the rich German nobles had lost interest in their grandiose project of creating a model German state in the New World.

German Settlements between 1848 and 1860

The demise of the Adelsverein in no way slowed down German immigration to Texas; rather, the movement continued to gain impetus with each passing year, and only the Civil War brought it to a momentary standstill. During this period the immigrants concentrated in two regions of the state. Apart from many who remained in major cities—San Antonio, Austin, Galveston, and Houston—between 1848 and 1860 most of the Germans settled in the Hill Country or near the older German settlements in the Brazos and Colorado valleys. The counties which received the majority of these later arrivals were Comal, Gillespie, Kendall, and Kerr in the west, and Fayette and Lee in the east.

The Western Counties

The western region, which became Kendall and Kerr Counties, was a beautifully rolling woodland with limestone outcroppings. The earliest settlement here was a "Latin Colony" called Sisterdale. Its existence actually dated from 1847 when Nikolas Zink, an eccentric Bavarian engineer who had reputedly built roads for the Greeks during their revolution, settled in the valley of the Sister Creeks, near their confluence with the Guadalupe River. He was followed by Ottomar von Behr, son of the prime minister of Anhalt-Köthen and an acquaintance of Bettina von Arnim and the scientist Alexander von Humboldt. Next came Julius Dresel, son of a wine exporter and a member of a prominent family in the German freedom movement. Then arrived the family of Dr. Ernst Kapp, the geography professor, who tested his theories of environment and technology on the frontier. His nephew Friedrich Kapp joined him in Texas before the younger Kapp became prominent in the national Republican Party during Lincoln's campaign and administration.

The names of those who followed the early Forty-Eighters sound like a *Who's Who* in German education and popular politics. Duke Paul of Württemberg found Sisterdale a quiet stopping place on his incessant journeys of exploration, which he undertook, some said, to avoid his nagging wife. Frederick Law Olmsted visited the settlement and marveled at a level of culture and sophistication such as he had not found elsewhere in the South.

41

Nikolas Zink's cabin at Sisterdale: the start of a Latin Colony

Their rude cabins, Olmsted noted, were stocked with fine paintings, books, and musical instruments. They conducted weekly meetings in Latin, mystifying their neighbors and creating the name "Latin Colonies" for the small settlement areas. Many of these immigrants found themselves unsuited to farm life in an austere environment and made their way to San Antonio and other towns. Sisterdale dwindled to a quiet country crossroads.

In 1852 three families departed from New Braunfels and traveled up the Guadalupe River into the backwoods of the Hill Country. This farming settlement on Cypress Creek above its confluence with the Guadalupe grew quickly, and in 1854 a young German developer named Ernst Hermann Altgelt laid out the town of Comfort there. The availability of farmland in the valleys and of ranchland in the hills, with abundant lumber and waterpower, made the transition from farming to ranching irresistibly appealing. Here also a sawmill was built, and lumbering soon became a vital part of the local economy.

As intellectuals and freethinkers gravitated toward the area around Comfort, the settlement grew to become another of the state's predominantly German towns. Emma Murck Altgelt, wife of Ernst, wrote in her colorful autobiography that "a kind of local government was slowly developed in Comfort. The citizens elected from their own a justice of the peace, a policeman, and other officials. When the children had grown to school age, it was decided to build a schoolhouse. One citizen donated the site. Others cut down oak trees, which others in turn hauled to the site. Beautiful cypress trees supplied the shingles for the roof. A blockhouse was soon finished. A teacher was found too. The little barefoot Comforters did not get too learned, but they grew up to be strong, healthy, and full of life, skilled in work about the house and the field, full of courage and love for riding and hunting, self-reliant with good practical sense, lords of creation clothed in skimpy garments." [34]

The Eastern Counties

While Sisterdale and Comfort were being settled in the western region of the German belt, many new communities were growing up in the eastern counties as well. This phase of German immigration into Fayette and Lee Counties coincided with the arrival in Texas of several ethnic minorities from German-speaking

Theodore Wiedenfeld, founder of the Cypress Creek Settlement, was a Freemason and community leader. The pattern in which settlers followed the Wiedenfelds to the valley tells an interesting story of interrelationships among the German Texans. Here again, ties of kinship and family letters reinforced the dominant role of "trailblazer" personalities.

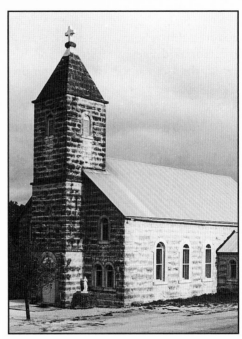

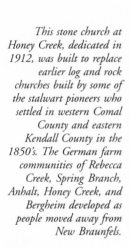

This stone church at Honey Creek, dedicated in 1912, was built to replace earlier log and rock churches built by some of the stalwart pioneers who settled in western Comal County and eastern Kendall County in the 1850's. The German farm communities of Rebecca Creek, Spring Branch, Anhalt, Honey Creek, and Bergheim developed as people moved away from New Braunfels.

Europe. These were the Czechs, Wends, and Poles. While these other groups usually established their own separate settlements, they sometimes mingled with their German neighbors so that today the ethnic distinctions seem somewhat blurred.

This part of the state had been settled by Anglo-Americans a generation before the first German communities were organized. Fayetteville, for example, in eastern Fayette County, had been founded about 1822 by several families from Austin's original colony. As German farmers moved into this fertile area, they tended to buy up the land which had been settled by the earlier Americans, while the Anglos, in turn, moved on. In this manner Fayetteville evolved into an Anglo-American and German community. Later, when the Czechs, or Bohemians, began to arrive, they too bought land from the original Anglo-American farmers, so, by the outbreak of the Civil War, Fayetteville had only a small Anglo-American element. Round Top, La Grange, and Giddings underwent similar transitions. The population of Fayette County consequently shifted from Anglo-American to German and Czech, while the population of Lee County went from Anglo-American to German and Wendish (a Germanicized Slavic nationality from Lusatia, an eastern European province governed by Prussia at the time the Wends left).

Since the area had been settled longer, life for European colonists throughout the eastern counties of Texas was never as difficult nor as dangerous as the region west of New Braunfels. As a result, the Germans in the east soon prospered. Furthermore, their commercial activities encouraged them to mix much more freely with non-German elements of the population than the Germans in the western counties did at first. Thus life in Victoria, DeWitt, Lavaca, Colorado, Austin, Fayette, Washington, and Lee Counties acquired a unique charm with the blending of rural traditions from the Old South and those of the European homeland.

Patterns of German Settlement after the Civil War

The federal blockade of Confederate ports during the Civil War effectively halted immigration into Texas. After the Civil War, however, immigration entered a new phase as increasing numbers of Germans filtered into the state. While the German belt extending across Central Texas absorbed most of these later immigrants, a significant number of them settled in small German folk-islands scattered across wide areas of South, North Central, and Northwest Texas. The German-speaking population of the state's developing cities—Houston, Austin, San Antonio, and Dallas—also increased considerably during the final decades of large-scale German immigration to Texas.

Many of the Germans who settled in the cities during the 1860's, 1870's, and 1880's were skilled artisans and craftsmen with no farming experience in Europe; large numbers of German intel-

Round Top in Fayette County was originally an Anglo-American settlement. As the first settlers moved out, German farmers came and stayed.

45

lectuals and proletarian freedom-fighters also settled in the urban areas. The impact of all these people on the growing cities of Texas was, in some cases, quite considerable. The 1850 census of the fledgling city of Houston showed a German-speaking element comprising 45 percent of the inhabitants. By the end of Reconstruction, the Germans no longer accounted for such a large part of the city's population, but they had become thoroughly established in mercantile enterprises and contributed much to local economic growth. Germans were active in Houston municipal politics; in cultural, religious, and Volksfest celebrations; in fraternal and fire-fighting organizations; and, significantly, in the city's wholesale liquor and saloon trade. [35]

Even in established centers like Galveston and San Antonio, as well as in other developing cities such as Austin and Dallas, the German population exerted an influence on local life far greater than its percentage of the urban population would suggest. Especially after the Civil War, their influence increased in local and state politics. During Reconstruction many of the state's leading German families won general acceptance into the political and social elite of Texas. Many of them had been Unionists, and, of course, they got the government jobs.

A large part of the German influx in the 1870's and thereafter came from other states in the Union. For example, in 1873 a group of Hessian artisans moved from New Orleans to a small settlement at Garland on Duck Creek, 13 miles north of Dallas, and within a year had established their own church with a missionary pastor from Missouri. The 1880's showed a marked movement of Germans from established communities of the central German belt of Texas into other less populous areas.

The advent of windmills in Texas made arid regions of the state feasible for agriculture, and German farmers started to settle the divides and plains of West Texas, making the transition from farming to ranching. The railroad companies often placed land on the market and offered free transportation as an inducement to settlers. In this fashion the community of Germania came into being in 1880 in Midland County. Today, however, the town has dwindled to a population of less than 30 and is known as "Paul" as a result of World War I hostility toward German Texans.

In 1889 one of the last significant colonization plans for settling Germans in Texas got under way in North Texas. It, too, was supported by railroad development. The first settlement created by this colonization plan was Muenster, located about 14 miles west of

Gainesville on the Missouri, Kansas, and Texas Railroad in present Cooke County. Muenster was established by the Flusche brothers, a group of enterprising young men from Westphalia. The Flusches were not beginners in this type of work; they had already started three successful colonies of German Catholics in Iowa and Kansas.

The brothers had initially intended to establish their fourth colony in Oklahoma, but they were told that the land they wanted had been reserved for French settlers. At that point they happened upon a letter written by a boyhood friend from Westphalia in the German Catholic newspaper *Amerika*, which was printed in St. Louis. This letter addressed the advantages of German settlement in North Texas. The brothers set out immediately for this region, where they found the perfect combination of conditions: a mild climate, a railroad which was eager to open land for settlement along a new line, and some ranchers who were equally eager to sell out for cash. The town of Muenster thrived with the establishment of a bank, a gin, a cheese plant, a flour mill, an oil refinery, and a newspaper. Two years later, in 1891, the Flusches founded their fifth German Catholic colony at Lindsay, a few miles east of Muenster in Cooke County.

Later that same year, the last movement to settle Catholics of German extraction in Texas began in St. Louis. This plan led to

Charles Philipp Axe (1831-1898) came to Louisiana about 1847. Although he was a tailor, he opened a wheelwright and blacksmith shop in New Orleans. Sixteen years later he led a group of relatives by boat to Galveston; from there they traveled to Duck Creek (now Garland) near Dallas. He and his brother Ludwig established the first German churches in Garland and Dallas.

47

August, Emil, and Anton Flusche

the establishment of Windthorst in Archer County under the religious leadership of Father Joseph Reisdorff, another indefatigable colonizer in North Texas, who later assisted with the founding of Rhineland (Knox County) in 1895, Nazareth (Castro County) in 1902, Umbarger (Randall County) in 1909, and Slaton (Lubbock County) in 1911.

Apart from a scheme spearheaded by a minister from Wisconsin to create a health resort and gardening center at Deutschburg near Matagorda Bay, three other interesting episodes remain in the history of German colonization in Texas before World War I.

One of these began halfway around the world in the farming village of Rorbach near the Black Sea. This part of the Ukraine, ruled by Imperial Russia, had been a vast domain with sparsely populated regions in 1762 when the German-born Czarina Catherine II launched her scheme to transplant German-speaking artisans and peasants into the Volga River Valley and the underdeveloped region of the Ukraine around the Black Sea. For a hundred years, these German Russians had lived a secluded but fairly good life in the Ukraine, where they were exempted by special imperial decrees from military service and regular taxation. As further inducement the Empress Catherine had even guaranteed full religious freedom, autonomy in local government, specified amounts of free land, and free transportation from Germany to Russia. Many of these privileges were withdrawn under later emperors, however, beginning in 1860, thus initiating a mass exodus of Russian Germans and Jews. In 1871 the exemption from compulsory military service was withdrawn, and in 1890 Russian became a required subject in the German schools. Together with several bad crop failures, these conditions precipitated a severe unrest among these Russian Germans and Russian Jews. In large numbers the Germans departed Russia for new homes in the Midwest, California, the Pacific Northwest, Canada, and Texas. In the early 1890's, a group of Black Sea German families bearing the names of Bachmann, Feiock, Fuhrmann, Graf, Hoeffner, Kafer, Moser, Obermeier, Oster, Ridinger, and Wust bought land at Hurnville, ten miles north of Henrietta in Clay County. This group was followed by a party of Volga Germans who settled in Lipscomb County in the Panhandle.

Another episode in the history of German colonization in Texas involved the settlement of German Lutherans in southwestern Haskell and eastern Stonewall Counties where the towns of Brandenburg (renamed "Old Glory" during World War I) and Sagerton developed in 1903 and 1905.

Still another episode of settlement began in 1905 when a congregation of German-speaking Mennonites was organized in Tuleta in Bee County. The Mennonites, part of a predominantly Swiss-German sect of 16th century Anabaptist origin, had a long history of persecution, being driven from country to country in search of religious and military freedom. Another Mennonite group from Ohio and Kansas, numbering over a hundred persons, settled temporarily in Dimmit County between 1911 and 1914. The next year a still larger body established a colony near Littlefield in Lamb County, northwest of Lubbock. In the 1930's and 1940's, the Mennonites increased their activities in South Texas, where they had established ten missions and congregations by 1957.

From Friedrich Ernst's exultant letter in 1832 to the arrival of the first Adelsverein ships in 1844, and from the collapse of Bettina in 1848 to the coming of the Russian Germans in the 1890's and the Mennonites in the 20th century, the immigrant story is a saga of common people with uncommon dreams.

The loss of ideals and the rebirth of hope were prevailing experiences of 19th century German colonists in Texas. Their departure from the Old World and their part in a struggle to push forward the edge of civilization is a story of broken homes, lost friends, and separation from known surroundings. For some it began as a tale of tragedy. "This was the first grave in Texas of a dearly beloved one for whom we mourned," wrote Ottilie Fuchs Goeth after her sister's death. "So soon then, we were bound to this country in such a way that, as Wilhelm von Humboldt put it, we associated home with two worlds." [36]

But they won out and made for themselves a new world in their own image. With the pride of youth, they boasted of young America. "There is not a potentate on earth who could conquer these United States! The immigrants have accepted the spirit of the Americans. The best thing about Americans," Carl Hilmar Guenther proclaimed, "is that they can strut before the whole world, for the country itself can supply everything it needs." [37]

They brought their past with them. They trusted that in their new world "everything would take root" and grow bigger and better than before. They were seekers pursuing a dream.

ERNST KAPP
The Desire to Be Free

*O*ne visitor to Professor Ernst Kapp's home on the frontier recalled that "within his book-covered walls he used to
serve his guests with self-grown wine and home-grown
tobacco," while he philosophized about "the advantages of life in the
country."

The professor was recognized by European scholars for two
works: a comparative cultural geography and a philosophy of tools
and technology. In these works Kapp foresaw, a century ahead of his
time, that mankind's development was shaped more by environment
than by history. The future as Kapp saw it was threatened by pollu-
tion and dehumanization in man's search for better machines to do
his work.

After a prison sentence in Germany resulting from his advo-
cating a more liberal government, Ernst Kapp took his family to
Texas, where they experimented with what he theorized was the
"perfect" way of life. The "free earth" of Texas overwhelmed the
professor's brave wife as the family journeyed inland; writing home,
she described a strange, psychic landscape in which fear of the unknown mingled with the temptation to see what lay ahead.
"Everybody tries to stop you by painting the next succeeding region

as horrifying, but up to now, as far as we have come, the land has become more and more beautiful. I find that one is overcome with an amazing change; the farther one comes inland, the more civilization ceases."

While the professor cleared the farm, wrote, and experimented with natural cures for physical illnesses, his wife told of the change which had come over him. "How contented, healthy, and happy Ernst here is. Daily he extols how fortunate it is for him that he came away from tired old Europe."

The whole family, in Ida Kapp's words, seemed transformed by the new surroundings and infected with energy and purpose. "If someone portrayed life the way we here are living it—we sleep with a cover and a pillow on the floor of a semifurnished room, do our cooking with one pot, one cauldron, and one cornbread pan for which we have to build a fire out in the yard, etc. Eating and drinking utensils consist of a few tin plates and tin cups; we have rented an ordinary kitchen table. For chairs we use baskets and trunks. Yes, would someone have portrayed it to me, I would have laughed. And yet I don't know how it happens, but I never before have been more content and in better health. I now have the courage to tackle any and all things and I know now that everything will take root." [38]

John Durst

George W. Smyth

GERMAN TRAILBLAZERS
The Durst Brothers and George Washington Smyth

*I*n the early 1800's, three brothers, Joseph, John, and Jacob Durst, entered Texas from Natchitoches, Louisiana. Born of German immigrant parents in Spanish Missouri, each of the three left a sharp imprint on Texas. Joseph, the oldest, was *alcalde* (mayor) of Nacogdoches in 1826. He was active in the Texas Revolution and later in Indian affairs of the Texas Republic until his death in 1843.

John Durst became the protégé and heir of wealthy Samuel Davenport, merchant and landowner at Nacogdoches. When Davenport died, leaving Durst his Texas properties, the young man became one of Texas's wealthiest citizens. He operated from Davenport's headquarters in the Old Stone Fort at Nacogdoches. Three years later he was elected to the Coahuila y Tejas legislature. At Monclova (the provincial capital), he was warned of Santa Anna's plans to invade Texas and, with an incredible horseback ride, reached home with the report in twelve and a half days. During the revolution this Texas "Paul Revere" commanded troops in East Texas.

The third brother, Jacob Darst, retained the original spelling of the family name. He was living at Gonzales at the outset of the Texas Revolution. When Mexican troops came there to demand the return of a cannon, the settlers buried it; later Jacob and two others dug it up for use against the Mexican army. On March 1, 1836, Jacob Darst joined 32 men from Gonzales who went to the relief of the Alamo. He was killed in the fortress six days later.

George Washington Smyth, son of a German millwright, came to Texas from Tennessee early in 1830. He settled at Nacogdoches, taught school, became a surveyor, and attained wide influence as a public figure. He represented his district at the Convention of 1836, signed the Texas Declaration of Independence, then joined his family in the Runaway Scrape. He served in the congress of the Texas Republic, as commissioner of the General Land Office, and as a member of the United States Congress. He died while serving as a delegate to the state's Constitutional Convention of 1866 after the Civil War.

TEXAS AND THE REVOLUTION
German Texians in War

*O*ne dramatic personal account of the Texas Revolution was published, not in Texas nor in the United States, as one would expect, but in Germany. *Texas und seine Revolution* was the work of Hermann Ehrenberg, a 17-year-old adventurer who landed in Texas in time to fight in San Antonio at the Siege of Béxar late in 1835. Early the next year, he and six German friends were with Fannin's ill-fated army at Goliad, when the entire command was captured and condemned to death. Three of the Germans, including Ehrenberg, were spared from the massacre and eventually released by the Mexicans. Ehrenberg returned to Germany six years later and became a teacher of English at the University of Halle, where he edited a journal of his experiences in the Texas Revolution and completed an account of the founding of the Lone Star Republic.

A yearning for the Wild West brought Ehrenberg back to the United States in later years. He settled this time in Arizona, where he found employment as a surveyor, mapmaker, road builder, and mining engineer. Mystery clouds his end. A story made its way back to his friends that he was attacked by Indians at an isolated stage stop

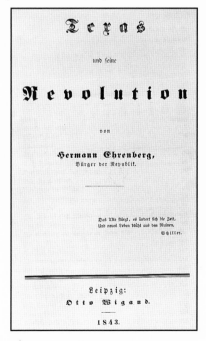

55

east of present-day Palm Springs, California, but strong suspicion persists that he was slain by the stationmaster for the large sum of money he carried. Ehrenberg was buried at the scene by his friend Mike Goldwater, a noted Arizona pioneer who subsequently named the town of Ehrenberg for him.

When the call went out in the fall of 1835 for Americans to aid in the revolt against Mexico, one young German immigrant in Kentucky was quick to enlist as a drummer in a volunteer company. Immanuel Frederick Gibenrath quickened the steps of these troops on the long trail to Texas, but, in less than six months, Gibenrath had fallen in the bloody massacre at Goliad. Quite some time later, his young widow and two daughters in Germany, awaiting word to come to America, finally learned of the death of the German drummer.

Another German who died in action in the fight for Texas independence was Gustav Bunsen. This was apparently the only time that Bunsen was on a winning side. A schoolteacher in Frankfurt and cousin of the inventor of the Bunsen burner, Gustav had taken part in the abortive Frankfurt *Putsch*, or coup, of 1833 and fled to the United States in the company of close associates. He belonged to a group called the Dreissiger because they were political refugees of the 1830's. With a couple of friends, Bunsen insisted on coming to Texas, despite warnings that the disease-ridden land was uninhabitable, filled with wild beasts and savage natives.

At least four other Germans fought with General Houston at San Jacinto. The best known of this group was Robert Kleberg, founder of Cat Spring. With him at San Jacinto were John Karner, Christian Wertzner, and Frederick Lemsky, who, tradition says, played the fife to signal the advance.

A LETTER TO FIRE THE IMAGINATION
From the Father of German Immigration to Texas

Settlement on Mill Creek, in Austin's Colony,
State of Texas, Republic of Mexico,
February 1, 1832.

In February of the previous year, we embarked on a brig to
New Orleans. It was still winter on our departure from New York,
then mild spring breezes blew upon us four days after our departure.
Between Cuba and Florida, we had later real summer, and the whole
sea voyage of a thousand miles over that part of the ocean, through
the Bahama Islands, into the Gulf of Mexico, up to the mouth of the
Mississippi, we lay constantly against the wind and came somewhat
back. On the Mississippi up to New Orleans, a hundred and twenty
miles (five make a German mile), we received favorable news of
Austin's colony in Texas; we embarked again in the schooner of
thirty-seven tons and landed after an eight-day voyage at Harris-
burgh in this colony.

Each immigrant who wishes to engage in farming receives a
league of land; a single person, one-quarter of a league. A league of
land contains four thousand four hundred and forty acres of land,
mountain and valley, woods and meadows, cut through by brooks.

The ground is hilly and alternates with forest and natural
grass plains. Various kinds of trees. Climate like that of Sicily. The
soil needs no fertilizer. Almost constant east wind. No winter, almost
like March in Germany. Bees, birds, and butterflies the whole winter
through. A cow with a calf costs ten dollars. Planters who have seven
hundred head of cattle are common. Principal products: tobacco,
rice, indigo grow wild; sweet potatoes, melons of an especial good-
ness, watermelons, wheat, rye, vegetables of all kinds; peaches in
great quantity grow wild in the woods, mulberries, many kinds of
walnuts, wild plums, persimmons sweet as honey; wine in great
quantity but not of a particular taste; honey is found chiefly in hol-
low trees. Birds of all kinds, from pelicans to hummingbirds. Wild
prey such as deer, bears, raccoons, wild turkeys, geese, partridges (the
latter as large as domestic fowls) in quantity. Free hunting and
fishing. Wild horses and buffalo in hordes; wolves, but of a feeble
kind; also panthers and leopards, of which there is no danger; rich
game, delicious roasts. Meadows with the most charming flowers.

Many snakes, also rattlesnakes; each planter knows safe means against them.

English the ruling speech. Clothing and shoes very dear. Each settler builds . . . a blockhouse. The more children, the better for . . . field labor. Scarcely three months work a year. No need for money, free exercise of religion, and the best markets for all products at the Mexican harbors; up the river there is much silver, but there are still Indian races there. We men satisfy ourselves with hunting and horseraces.

On account of the yellow fever, one should arrive some weeks before the month of July or after the first of October. It is a good thing if one can speak English; only enough money is needed as is necessary to purchase a league of land. A father of a family must remember that he receives on his arrival, through the land granted to him, a small kingdom which will come to be worth in a short time from seven to eight hundred [dollars], for which it is often sold here. The expenses for the land need not be paid immediately. Many raise the money from their cattle.

Your friend,
Friedrich Ernst

N.B. Passports are not necessary. Sons over seventeen have like part in the settlement of the land.

HOW A BRIDE WAS WON

*C*aroline Louise Sacks von Roeder, mother of Mrs. Robert Justus Kleberg, gave the following account of the rambunctious life and the "bittersweet wedding of our wild son Sigismund, whose duel with the Prince of Prussia brought us all to Texas."

"About a dozen young men met at the house of Benjamin Buckingham on the Brazos. This young Kentuckian had recently brought his young bride to his plantation, and they were all celebrating. The men drifted into cards. Soon the losers dropped out. Sigismund was most favored, Buckingham was losing—the game narrowed to these two. When Buckingham's cash was gone, he put up his bills of sale for his mules, workhorses, yokes of oxen. Then, one by one, Buckingham's slaves came into the game. Sigismund raked in the bills of sale.

"With his personal property gone, Buckingham sent for the title papers to the various plots on his plantation. Buckingham lost. Then he looked around the room—his bride entered. He then drew his marriage certificate from his pocket, 'We'll play for that!' Instantly Sigismund pushed his winnings into the middle of the table. 'Certainly we will, but not without the consent of the lady.' She smiled; they played, Buckingham lost. As Sigismund rose to consolidate the marriage certificate with his other winnings, Buckingham fired but missed, and as he reached for another pistol, Sigismund flashed his sword (the same that had killed the Prince of Prussia) and ran him through. The Coroner found self-defense. In a loud, ringing voice, the same official was heard to say, 'Will you, Barbara Buckingham, take this man . . . ?'

"Dear sister: Was ever woman in this humor wooed? Was ever woman in this manner won?

"Hurry, hurry and join us. Texas is truly the land of freedom and romance."

From Dorothy E. Justman,
German Colonists and Their Descendants in Houston

FERDINAND LINDHEIMER
Father of Botany in Texas

*F*erdinand Lindheimer (1801-1879) from Frankfurt was certainly one of the most diversified of German settlers in Texas. Lindheimer, son of a wealthy merchant and a relative of Goethe, had been a close friend of the Bunsens and had worked as a botany teacher at the Bunsen Institute, which the authorities suspected was training German revolutionaries. Immediately after the failure of the Frankfurt *Putsch*, he escaped to the United States and settled in the "Latin" village of Belleville, Illinois, across the Mississippi River from St. Louis. From there, in 1834, the adventurous Lindheimer flatboated with five friends down the river to New Orleans, where they intended to provision themselves for an expedition into Texas. The promise, however, of taking part in a Mexican uprising evidently lured three of them to Veracruz. For the next 16 months, Lindheimer was variously employed in Mexico as distiller on a coffee plantation and as overseer on a banana and pineapple plantation. He still found time, though, to make an extensive collection of insects and plants.

In the last months of 1835, Lindheimer was caught up in the Texas Revolution. Because of his hatred for political oppression, he supposedly declined a commission in the army of Santa Anna and started for Texas: "I recognized that this was the moment to carry out my original plan of going to Texas before the decisive battle." Shipwrecked near Mobile, Lindheimer joined Houston's army one day after the Battle of San Jacinto.

Lindheimer remained in Texas as a botanical collector until 1839, when he returned to St. Louis to work out an arrangement with Dr. Asa Gray of Harvard University for extensive botanical investigation in Texas. Back in Texas in 1843, Lindheimer bought a two-wheeled, horse-drawn cart and a supply of pressing paper, flour, coffee, and salt, and set out with two dogs. The trips often lasted as long as a month as Lindheimer explored the Brazos, Colorado, and Guadalupe River valleys. On one of these trips, he made the acquaintance of Reverend Louis Cachand Ervendberg, whom Prince Solms had invited to become pastor of the Adelsverein colony, and through this association Lindheimer became the prince's guide into the wilderness.

His colleague, the paleontologist-geologist Roemer, leaves this sketch of Lindheimer: "At the end of the town, some distance from the last house, half hidden beneath a group of elm and oak

Texas Prickly-pear
Opuntia lindheimeri

Lindheimer had organized the plants of Texas into a system by 1851. About 20 species of plants and one genus of Texas wildflowers honor his name today and recall his contributions to American science. Pictured is the Texas prickly pear, or Opuntia lindheimeri.

Lindheimer's log cabin in New Braunfels

trees, stood a hut or little house close to the banks of the Comal. It furnished an idyllic picture with its enclosed garden and general arrangement and position. When I neared this simple, rustic home, I spied a man in front of the entrance busily engaged in splitting wood. Apparently he was used to this kind of work. He wore a blue jacket, open at the front, yellow trousers, and the coarse shoes customarily worn by farmers in the vicinity. It was the botanist, Mr. Ferdinand Lindheimer. He acquired for himself an enduring reputation through his many years of assiduous collecting of plants and through his study of the botany of Texas, which up to this time was almost unknown." By 1851 Lindheimer had organized the plants of Texas into a system. About 20 species of plants and one genus of Texas wildflowers honor his name today and recall his contributions to American science.

During the Civil War, Lindheimer took a moderate political position. As editor of the *Neu-Braunfelser Zeitung*, which he founded in 1852, Lindheimer attacked German unionism because he clearly saw that it would lead to trouble between German colonists and Anglo-American settlers. Furthermore, he counseled his native countrymen to fall in step with American life but exhorted them to keep their language and culture on the edge of a savage wilderness. Lindheimer's paper influenced German settlers for nearly a quarter of a century. After Lindheimer retired, the paper continued German publication until 1957.

Ferdinand Lindheimer

TWO VIEWS OF IMMIGRATION. Which one was true? Were they both accurate? Or did it depend on each person's outlook? In the end, wasn't one person's hell another's paradise?

Oh, you poor Germans! my dear countrymen! if you in your old homeland only knew what is awaiting you in Texas under the auspices and guidance of the Society, you would desist with a sense of horror and trembling from your decision to emigrate to Texas, and you would remain in your dear fatherland!

Carl Blumberg

We are now quite content and happy. When one gets adjusted, that is, has his house finished and field fenced, it is a better living here than that of a farmer in Europe. I have no desire ever to go back. Whoever wants to see must come here; I do not believe that he will regret it.

Hubert Lux

Whosoever wants to come would do well to bring iron, copper, and tin house and kitchen utensils, spade and hoes, a pan for cleaning fruits, and a plow (since the domestic plows are not as good as the German plows). Bring a pair of wheels for a cart and also a grind-stone. Bring garden seeds and summer wheat. Whosoever comes must never allow himself to be detained on the coast by Americans nor by Germans who being too lazy to work have fallen victims to drunkenness or lead some other dissolute life. But come up to here . . . where fever and other sicknesses never occur.

Hubert Lux

DR. FERDINAND ROEMER

*O*ne of the most valuable surveys of Texas flora, fauna, and geology was published in Germany in 1849. The book *Texas* by Ferdinand Roemer has since been translated and republished several times. This young German paleontologist was sent by the Berlin Academy of Science to make a geological survey of Texas, in particular the area within the Adelsverein grant. Roemer was a keen observer and a diligent worker. His letter of introduction from Alexander von Humboldt read, "Dr. Roemer, like a book, needs but to be opened to yield good answers to all questions." In gathering his scientific specimens, he was greatly aided by the children of the German settlements, who regarded him as their friend. After more than a year of exploration, he returned to Germany, where he produced a book bearing the simple title *Texas*. This volume is important not only for its wealth of information about the natural setting, but also for its penetrating insights into the society of the times and the opportunities afforded by this new land.

"I have noticed irregularity and romanticism in regard to the clothing of the young German colonists recently come to Texas. It seems as if they wanted to compensate themselves . . . for the restraint which the manners and customs of the homeland had imposed upon them. The almost total absence of cultured women also helped to encourage this recklessness in dress.

"The clothing of my companions was a particular object of attention to me. They could hardly have been more fantastic and heterogeneous if they had been taken from the wardrobe of a theater. The component parts were borrowed from the Indian, the Mexican, the American, and the German costumes, but the greater part was a production to suit the capricious taste of the individual.

"The colonist who has not farmed in the Old Country must have an unusual amount of endurance and willpower. I have seen quite a few German peasants and laborers, who had come here without any funds, come into possession of little farms through their industry. These supplied them with the necessities of life and even gave promise of future affluence and comfortable living. On the other hand, I have hardly seen ten people of the higher class, supplied with moderate funds, who within a year were able to acquire a house with a fenced-in field and of whom one could hope that they would be able to sustain themselves through their own efforts."

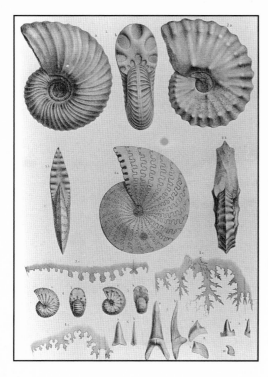

Fossils from Roemer's Kreidebildungen von Texas

Roemer's affection for Texas is evidenced in the concluding lines of his book *Texas*: "During my stay of more than a year, I had grown to love the beautiful land of meadows, to which belongs a great future. It moved me to sorrow that I must say farewell. . . . To me there still remain rich and pleasant memories; and from afar I shall always follow with lively interest the further development of the country. May its broad, green prairies become the habitation of a great and happy people."

The Vereinskirche served triple duty in early Fredericksburg as a house of worship, school, and fortress. Dr. William Hermes comments: "Before Meusebach made the treaty with the Comanche Indians at the San Saba, the Fredericksburg colonists lived in fear of attack by Indians and had organized themselves into a mounted company and a foot company for the defense of the colony. A shot from the cannon was to be a signal for all colonists to assemble armed in the marketplace before the municipal building."

"Remove not the ancient landmarks which your fathers have set."
(Proverbs 22:28)

The old Marienkirche at Fredericksburg—
Building the great stone church was a three-year struggle of major proportions. Begun in 1860 to replace the earlier Catholic church of 1849, the construction went ahead by fits and starts. The tasks of quarrying, stonecutting, lime burning, hauling sand and lumber, measuring and staking off the foundation, masonry, carpentry, and plastering were undertaken by the townspeople. "Even children helped by carrying water," explained Fredericksburg historian Ella Gold. "At times work came to a standstill, for field-work and other jobs had to be done." As the work continued into the Civil War, "some workmen were obliged to exchange the hammer and trowel for weapons of war. Building materials and even food were often in short supply since freighters were in service of the Confederacy. Ofttimes a pall of sadness hung over the community because of Civil War horror and Indian atrocities. Not all who labored at this church construction lived to see it finished."

Sunday House

BUILDING A WORLD
An Essay in Pictures

*T*he frontier settlements never became "farm villages" in the German sense, because farmers lived outside the towns, which became commercial and social centers for the surrounding rural areas. On the weekends farm families traveled in wagons and buggies to town for marketing, social gatherings, and worship. During these visits they "camped out" in small weekend cottages, called Sunday Houses, built for this purpose in town. The stylized construction of these dwellings, found predominantly in Fredericksburg, consisted of three rooms on the ground floor, a front porch, and a wooden outside stairway leading on one side to an attic, where the children slept in a bedroom under the rafters.

Comfort

The first German settlers we saw we knew at once. They lived in little cabins and had enclosures of ten acres of land about them. The cabins were simple, but there were many little conveniences . . . and a care to secure comfort in small ways.

Frederick Law Olmsted

Fredericksburg has really progressed in the last few years, and only strong, well-built stone houses are built now.

Franz Kettner, 1856

*Windmill and tankhouse,
Cat Spring*

Herman Grobe farmhouse, Crabapple Community

*Bethlehem Lutheran Church,
Round Top*

*St. Joseph's Church,
San Antonio*

71

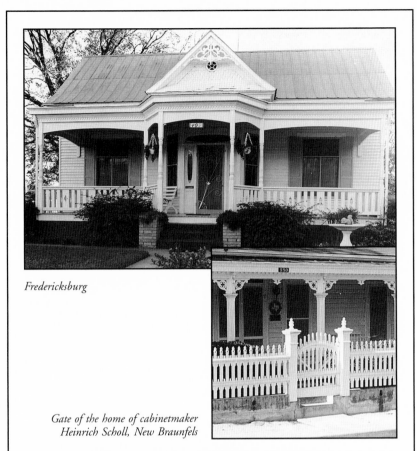

Fredericksburg

*Gate of the home of cabinetmaker
Heinrich Scholl, New Braunfels*

The bandstand on the Fredericksburg town square

Round Top

I never in my life, except perhaps in awakening from a dream, met with such a sudden and complete transfer of associations. Instead of loose-boarded or hewn-log walls with crevices stuffed with rags or daubed with mortar, which we have been accustomed to see during the last month, or staving in a door, where we have found any to open; instead, even, of four bare, cheerless sides of whitewashed plaster, which we have found twice or thrice only in a more aristocratic American residence, we were—in short, we were in Germany.

Frederick Law Olmsted

"I have seen a rich, beautiful world filled with resources, full of challenges for the industrious."

*T*he immigrants' eyes beheld a world vastly different from anything they had ever known before—a raw, uncivilized, untamed wilderness. Beneath its rough surface, however, they guessed that the land could produce great riches which would secure their future in the New World. What they suspected was indeed true, but only through great perseverance and industry did the land release its abundance.

With considerable wisdom and insight, Friedrich Wilhelm von Wrede wrote in 1844, "My observations do not show any strolls along rosy pathways. I have not seen any fried pigeons fly into anyone's mouth. However, I have seen a rich, beautiful world filled with resources, full of challenges for the industrious, with abundant and assured awards as far as this world can ever guarantee them." [39]

Although the American way of life, like the geography and climate, was strange to the German immigrants, they tried to some extent to fit into the American mold, but the German newcomers were generally better educated and more widely read than their American counterparts; they were tradition-bound and preferred their old ways to the new. To them, Americans were friendly, but also rambunctious and often vulgar. The Germans tended therefore to remain silent and apart from their new countrymen, without meaning to give offense, while, among their own people, they were fun-loving and outgoing.

At times, as the isolation seemed to increase, the Germans fell back on their old customs as a means of security against the loneliness of exile and became more "German" even than they had been in their homeland. This natural reaction was sometimes misinterpreted by the Anglo-Americans as aloofness, a deliberate attempt to shun American company.

One German writer understood the problems which arose on both sides. "The inhabitants intermingle little with Americans," she noted. "The Germans are not as enterprising as the latter, but they are steady and industrious." [40]

Not all German immigrants, however, found it so difficult to adjust to American culture. For those who came early or who settled in areas where few other Germans lived, the process of assimilation was easier; they necessarily lived more closely with Americans and had to change.

George B. Erath was one such individual who welcomed the new way of life with no reservations. "It was a bold dream, that of going to America from Austria. For Austria did not encourage emigration; she barely permitted it. Americans have been surprised at my association here with Americans alone, and regarding the German not as a fellow-countryman, but simply as another citizen of the United States or of Texas; but the fact is that I left the whole of that land, Germany and Austria, deeming that I owed no allegiance to either." [41]

For the majority of the Germans who, unlike Erath, settled in predominantly German Central Texas, it was the land—that raw wilderness—which created a bond with the American frontiersmen. Together they were undertaking the same bold mission—to create an "agrarian utopia of hardy and virtuous yeomen." [42] Strengthened later by business ties as the frontier developed into a modern state, this goal gave the immigrants and the Anglo-Americans a common purpose. On three occasions—the Civil War, World War I, and World War II—the bond was seriously tested, but it held and gave evidence of the colonists' social and economic assimilation.

The first obstacle to be overcome on the frontier was the ever-present danger of Indian attack. For generations during the westward movement, the Anglo-Americans had been engaged in a fierce struggle with the natives of the North American wilderness. Numerically outnumbered and otherwise vulnerable because they lacked frontier experience, the German Texans attempted a new solution to the old problem, when John O. Meusebach's peace mission secured a treaty of friendship with the Comanche chiefs in 1847. The treaty was essential to the success of German colonization plans because it afforded

August Faltin, banker and merchant, with his wife, Clara von Below

The Indian Treaty of 1847

the long-range stability required for the establishment of towns, businesses, and industry. In a direct way, it was effective in attracting investment capital and expertise to the frontier.

A young Prussian banker named August Faltin had far-reaching prospects in mind when he came to the Hill Country with his young wife, and the money he brought with him financed the growth of Comfort and Kerrville. Faltin was especially interested in helping mercantile businesses and industry get started. He invested in land development, in the construction of lumber- and gristmills, and in general merchandise stores such as the one established in Kerrville by Charles Schreiner after the Civil War.

Another sign of stability and prosperity in a frontier settlement was the water mill. Like the railroad a generation later, mills made life easier, and they attracted other businesses, especially freighting. Cities such as Victoria, La Grange, and Brenham already had flourishing mills when the Germans came into these areas; the Comal and Guadalupe Rivers at New Braunfels also afforded several excellent sites for saw-, textile-, and gristmills. But building a European water mill and keeping it running in the Texas Hill Country west of New Braunfels was difficult. Although German millers brought skill and experience to the Hill Country, their dependence upon the cantankerous environment required quite untraditional adaptations in order to keep a traditional mill in operation. Most of these millers served a second apprenticeship on the frontier.

One of the earliest mills in the Fredericksburg area was built in 1850 by Carl Hilmar Guenther from Saxony. Construction of this mill took more than six months. The waterwheel and driving gears were fashioned from native woods, and the buhrstones, or millstones, were imported from France. Guenther boasted in letters to his parents in Germany that this Live Oak Mill was a triumph of technology. A few weeks later, when floodwaters tore away his dam, Guenther had second thoughts about his adopted homeland. Stunned and disgusted, all he could write home was, "The Lord had other plans!"

If anything stood out in the personality of Carl Hilmar Guenther, who later founded Pioneer Flour Mills in San Antonio, it was a kind of dogged determination to succeed in whatever he set his mind to accomplish. When the damage had been repaired and a new dam had been built, "so strong that it would never be torn down again," he observed his work with pride. "After the mill was finished and I walked around the place, I thought of you very earnestly, dear Father. Completely lost in my musing, I looked up and saw the carpenter was tying a green live oak branch on the gable. That called for a celebration. We spent the evening gayly. I had gotten a small keg of wine from my neighbor. Things really cheered up under the four big live oak trees I have in the front yard. After the first few toasts, I

Christian Dietert,
master millwright

remembered my good parents who had so kindly furnished the money for this undertaking. We all joined in a 'Lebewohl' to them which resounded so heartily I felt you had to hear it even at that distance." [43]

Besides Guenther, another early Hill Country millwright was Nikolas Zink, the Bavarian engineer. Zink first laid out the streets of New Braunfels for Prince Solms, and then, with Christian Dietert and Michael Lindner, he planned the construction of two or three Hill Country mills.

Christian Dietert was another expert millwright who found it hard to second-guess the unruly Texas weather. In 1855 Dietert and Zink built the Perseverance Mill at Comfort. Mrs. Emma Murck Altgelt, whose husband financed the construction, called the project a "thankless undertaking." The first dam, "considered indestructible," washed away. Then a drought kept the mill idle during the next year. Dietert gave up and moved to Fredericksburg, where he no sooner finished a new mill than it was swept away by a flash flood. [44]

Figuring that he was now an expert on Texas floods and dry spells, Dietert gambled that his next mill would succeed. In 1857 he and a young millwright from Germany named Balthasar Lich erected a mill on the cliffs of the Guadalupe River at the lumbering and shingle-making camp of Kerrville. The river ensured ample water for continuous operation, and an ingenious low dam running diagonally across the river withstood floodwaters as long as Dietert lived.

During the four years between 1857 and 1861 when the Civil War broke out, the German towns thrived. Substantial houses had replaced the huts and cabins which the early settlers had hastily built upon arrival. Immigration had reached an all-time high, and the population of the towns and rural countryside rose sharply each year. Business especially had increased at a brisk pace. German mills supplied flour and lumber to cities such as San Antonio, and the demand for German craftsmen and clerks was high. German teamsters drove their wagons all over the state carrying raw produce from the thriving German communities and returning with goods and merchandise which the colonists could not make for themselves.

For a while, though, it looked as if the Civil War threatened to undo what the German immigrants and Anglo-Americans had struggled to accomplish together. For various complex reasons, many German Texans opposed both slavery and secession, and this opposition, which the Germans did little to hide, set them at odds with the majority of the rest of the state. Most Germans opposed slavery as a matter of principle and hoped that the institution would disappear. They believed, however, that the states could not solve the problem without federal financial assistance to help the plantation owners through the transition period. The small German farmers with their modest holdings and often limited capital had little use for slaves. The German intellectuals liked neither slavery nor the idea of disunion. Many of them had left Germany disillusioned because of the failure there to create a united German nation.

An insistence upon absolute human liberty was at the root of the antislavery fervor. Friedrich Kapp quickly perceived the universal implications of the issue. "The problem of slavery is not the problem of the Negro," he wrote. "It is the eternal conflict between a small privileged class and the great mass of the nonprivileged, the eternal struggle between aristocracy and democracy." [45] For Germans like Kapp, slavery was a contradiction of what America represented. Many idealistic Germans saw it as the destiny of the Germans and the Americans to reunite in the common struggle to extend the frontiers of human liberty. [46] In the North that ideal was not at all out of place; in the South in 1861, it was extremely dangerous.

Not all Germans took such an active stand against slavery. Ferdinand Lindheimer, editor of the *Neu-Braunfelser Zeitung*, wisely cautioned German Texans not to antagonize the Anglo-American settlers by meddling in their affairs. He warned that the problem was an old one and that the German newcomers perhaps did not understand all the issues. But Lindheimer also stood up for his German countrymen when English-language newspapers accused Germans of being traitors. As he clearly saw, the issue was not one which could be discussed logically; he understood better than most other German intellectuals that really two questions were at stake: slavery and the Union. Many Southerners besides the Germans, notably the venerable Sam Houston, opposed secession. Especially in the Texas frontier counties, many Anglo-Americans as well as Germans opposed secession because it would leave them without protection from the Indians.

Had more Germans heeded Lindheimer's counsel, the tragedy that followed might have been averted. Unionism was so strong in the freethinking villages of Sisterdale and Comfort that several hundred male Unionists organized a German battalion with companies from Kendall, Gillespie, and Kerr Counties on the Fourth of July 1862. When letters were intercepted allegedly connecting the German officers

Funeral of German Unionists at Comfort, August 20, 1865

with Southern Unionists such as A.J. Hamilton (later military governor of Texas) and E.J. Davis (last Reconstruction governor), these counties were declared in open rebellion and placed under strict martial law. Believing that a safe-conduct had been issued, the German cadre assembled for movement into Mexico but was ambushed by a Confederate force on the early morning of August 10, 1862. This Battle of the Nueces, as it came to be called, effectively crushed the idealism of the German-Texan Unionists. No one dared even to gather the bones of the fallen until after the war, when the remains were transported to Comfort and buried under an impressive obelisk which bears the inscription "Treue der Union" (Loyal to the Union), along with the names of the victims. Like the name of "Loyal Valley" northwest of Fredericksburg, this monument is one of the few remaining evidences of the German-Texan Unionists.

This Unionist uprising severely strained relations between the Germans and the Anglo-American majority. Ottilie Fuchs Goeth described the horrors of the "lynch law." "A few miles from Marble Falls, on the road to Johnson City, one can see a place where men favoring the North were killed and thrown into a cavern. Many of the best men of this area lost their lives at this spot. Gradually the men grew more cautious and at least gave the appearance of supporting the Confederates." [47]

"To the German colonies," wrote a somewhat overwrought August Siemering of Sisterdale, the war "had been like a nightmare. No more immigrants from Europe had come since 1860. On the contrary, thousands had left the state. A considerable number of them had settled in Mexico," where German life "was strengthened at that time by Austrian troops. Most of the German Texans went to the Northern states, where they enlisted in the army, or back to Germany," he exclaimed, speaking, of course, of his small circle of friends, the intellectual minority. "Many a house in Texas stood empty, and many a field remained uncultivated. The small places were empty, and in others there were only women and children left. When the Union flag was flying again on the capitol in Austin, the question was raised whether or not the Germans could find their home again in Texas." [48]

Despite this grim outlook, conditions improved considerably for the Germans during Reconstruction (1866-1874). They found that Texas was indeed a home for them. In many respects Reconstruction coincided with a boom in Texas agriculture and business. For the Germans there was also a "boom" in politics. Because many of them had been adamant Unionists and thus were able to take the "Ironclad Oath," thus permitting them to participate in politics, they were voted into a number of local, state, and federal offices. Governors like A.J. Hamilton and E.J. Davis did not forget that the Germans had stood alongside them when opposition to the Confederacy had been dangerous, and under their administrations Germans held a number of political appointments. For many Germans who became prominent during the last part of the 19th century, Reconstruction was their introduction to business, politics, and public life. In short, they became "practicing Americans" for the first time.

Within the state several developments contributed to an improvement in the standard of living during this boom in Texas history. The first extensive railroad connections between Texas and other states were laid in 1872, and manufacturing and commerce improved as a result. The population grew, and German immigration to Texas began again. Agriculture received an enormous boost, and cattle drives became larger and more profitable. Families like the Klebergs, the Reals, the Schreiners, and the Wilhelms, involved in cattle and sheep ranching and in investment, were part of this growth. Also helpful to the rising economy, Indian raids were declining rapidly, and after 1875 they ceased almost entirely. Here, too, German volunteers, militiamen, and rangers contributed their part by serving as frontier guards and civil lawmen.

Abroad, one major event helped to complete the Americanization of the German Texans. This, strangely enough, was the unification of Germany.

The unification in 1871 after Germany's victory over France in the Franco-Prussian War inspired great celebration in Texas. A German grandmother whose parents had been immigrants wrote that the German nationalistic anthem, "'The Watch on the Rhine,' had taken to the field, and the news of [German] victory spread around the world. We too heard the news and were surprised to read of the astonishing victories . . . with capture of Emperor Napoleon III. Then finally there came the renewal of the German Reich at Versailles. It was difficult to fathom, and one feared to be imagining it. Still it was true, and probably the reality was more meaningful than the papers related. Germany was an empire as large and grand as in the days of the Hohenstaufen. Young dreams had been fulfilled. Old people were glad to have survived long enough to have experienced it, even those living in Texas, where so many had fled from their fatherland because the political timepiece of Germania had run too slowly. And yet it had come about."

"Away then with the bloody revolutions of the 1840's. All were in accord, all praised the emperor. . . . Devotion to Bismarck was boundless. . . . In 1870, and later, I saw some letters written by German girls expressing regrets that they were not men in order to join in the battle. It was sincerely meant, so truly German, not just empty phraseology." [49]

Perhaps during the Franco-Prussian war more than at any other time, the older generation of German Texans longed for another glimpse of their homeland. But while they rejoiced at the long-awaited news of the new Germany, they sensed that the unification, achieved without them, left them no part in the old country. The land they had left no longer existed. It had become a new, modern nation, and, for the German Texans, there was no past to which they could return. They could only go forward into the future—as Americans.

With the rigors of the frontier behind and with a native-born generation growing to maturity, the German Texans set off in pursuit of the "American dream"—politically, financially, and socially. In the words of historian Joe Frantz, "the Germans joined with the newly freed slaves to support the Republican Party." Because they connected Democrats with the Confederacy, "the Germans became the backbone of the Republican Party in Texas and the cornerstone of the two-party system" in this state. [50] Several German Texans became especially prominent in public and political life during the decade following Reconstruction. Jacob Kuechler, who had come to Texas from the University of Giessen as a member of the Forty, had become a West Texas surveyor after the collapse of the settlements of Bettina and Tusculum. Then, after escaping from the German Unionist uprising, he had waited out the Civil War in Mexico. Upon returning to the state, he had become a delegate to the Constitutional Convention of 1868-1869. From 1870 until 1875, he served as commissioner of the General Land Office in Austin.

Gustav Schleicher from Darmstadt was another member of the Forty who rose to a position of leadership. Educated at Giessen in civil engineering and architecture, he worked in Texas as a millwright, surveyor, and politician. During the war he had held a commission in the Confederate Corps of Engineers. Later he practiced law in San Antonio and superintended the construction of the San Antonio and Mexican Gulf Railroad. Between 1875 and 1879, he served three terms in the United States House of Representatives.

One of the most distinguished German Texans during this period held no political positions at all; Dr. Ferdinand von Herff was a leader in Texas medicine. Already a famous surgeon at 27, Herff negotiated with the Adelsverein and was one of the leaders of the Forty to Texas. Here he became a proponent of gradual political re-

Gustav Schleicher

Ferdinand Ludwig von Herff—The son of a privy-councillor of Hesse-Darmstadt and a cousin of Meusebach, young Herff was acquainted with Alexander von Humboldt, Prince Frederick of Prussia, and a future czarina of Russia.

form and published a farsighted theory of politics in 1850. Later his home in San Antonio became a center for his advanced research in surgery and pathology. Herff studied cures for tuberculosis and performed plastic surgery, the first hysterectomy in this country, and the first cataract surgery in the state. Dr. Herff was also instrumental in developing a licensing program for young doctors in Texas. He finally retired from surgery at the age of 88.

Both Schleicher and Herff lived in San Antonio, where Germans had composed a third of the voting constituency in the 1850's. For the next 50 years, until the turn of the century, so many of the city's Republican politicians were Germans that one could say San Antonio was governed at times from the Casino Hall, the club of the German elite.

"The best-known case of the Germans' Republican consistency," in the words of Joe Frantz, "surfaces in the person of Harry M. Wurzbach, a San Antonio and Seguin lawyer. In Seguin, a heavily German town, Wurzbach, a Republican, served as county attorney and for four terms as county judge. In 1920 Wurzbach was elected to the United States Congress from the 14th Texas District, the first native Texas German to be a Republican representative. The Germans in the San Antonio-Seguin area combined with San Antonio's military to continue to elect him for four terms, again the first Republican from Texas to be elected more than two terms. The Germans voted as automatically for him as Boston's Irish voted for James J. Curley. . . . Wurzbach proved to be more than the 14th District's representative; he was the congressman for every German-descended Texan." [51]

Since Wurzbach's tenure in Congress in the 1920's, politicians running for statewide offices in Texas have had to reckon with the middle-of-the-road "German vote" of Gillespie, Mason, Kendall, Kerr, Comal, Guadalupe, DeWitt, and Washington Counties. In politics German voters favored candidates and platforms that were safe, conservative, but progressive. They also resisted attempts to legislate public conduct and morals. German voters never did approve of the national Prohibition movement. They voted it down in every election and ignored it when the amendment finally passed.

In addition to politics, the Germans of San Antonio pursued the "American dream" in retail business, manufacturing, and commerce. Like German Texans throughout the state, they were industrious. Also like other Germans, they consumed quantities of beer. Nearly every German town of consequence in Texas had at least one brewery; San Antonio had six major breweries and a number of smaller ones. Possibly the most famous beer in its time was Menger Beer. Brewed in a small building next door to the Alamo, the beer was nearly as well known as the historic shrine itself. William Menger, who operated this brewery in San Antonio after the mid-1840's, developed so much business from New Braunfels, Castroville, Seguin, and Fredericksburg that he needed a place to house his customers overnight. In 1859 he built the Menger Hotel adjacent to the Alamo. Later additions turned it into one of the city's most famous stopping places. Officers of various military units headquartered in San Antonio prized the fine food and excellent bar. Teddy Roosevelt is said to have done his most effective recruiting for the Rough Riders at the Menger Bar.

About the same time that Menger built his hotel, Friedrich Groos formed a partnership with his brothers Carl and Gustav to establish a small general merchandise firm that grew to become Groos National Bank in San Antonio. Another German San Antonian, H.W. Finck, was a cigar manufacturer. The Finck Cigar Company is the

The Menger Hotel

William Gebhardt (seated in the center)

only one of 18 earlier cigar factories in San Antonio still in existence in 1996; Finck's special "Travis Club" is marketed nationwide.

In 1896 William Gebhardt established a factory in the city to make chili powder. At the beginning they could make five cases a week; these were sold from the back of a wagon driven around town. Ultimately Gebhardt invented and patented 37 machines for his factory, and, following an expansion in 1911, the company put out the first canned chili con carne and tamales.

Other livelihoods in San Antonio derived from the state's growing agricultural industry. In 1859 Carl Hilmar Guenther moved his milling operations to San Antonio because of the city's growing population and because the state was producing increasingly larger quantities of wheat, which could otherwise be marketed only in the North and Midwest. Henry Schelper, like many others, based his living on the growing cattle industry. He began as a butcher after the Civil War, then opened a large meat market, and finally operated as a livestock broker and wholesaler at the San Antonio stockyards.

In many respects San Antonio is one example of what was happening to the urban German-Texan population during the last quarter of the 19th century. However, the basis of the economy that

*Henry Schelper —
San Antonio butcher and
member of the Casino
Club and Turn-Verein*

Hank Smith's rock house, 1877

sustained San Antonio's breweries, hotels, factories, and stockyards was the Texas livestock industry. In livestock raising too, German Texans made significant contributions as farmers and ranchers.

Born Heinrich Schmidt in 1836 in Germany, pioneer Hank Smith broke the first sod, planted the first crops, and dug the first well on the high plains of northwest Texas. At the opposite end of the state, Robert Justus Kleberg Sr. started a ranching dynasty. Kleberg had raised tobacco and served as chief justice of Austin County before he moved to DeWitt County in 1847 and served as chief justice in 1853 and 1855. He was a leading rancher in that area until his death in 1888. Twenty-five years later Kleberg County in South Texas was named for him. A son, Rudolph, served in the state senate before being elected to the United States Congress from 1896 to 1903. Today Robert Justus Kleberg's descendants own and operate the famous King Ranch, with 1,250,000 acres in Nueces, Kleberg, Kenedy, and Willacy Counties.

Several pioneer sheep raisers built ranching empires after the Civil War. Captain Charles Schreiner, a German-speaking Alsatian and a Texas Ranger, built his sheep flocks to 40,000 head. From his humble beginnings as a Kerrville shopkeeper financed by August Faltin, Schreiner acquired 600,000 acres in Kerr, Edwards, and Kimble Counties. Largely under his leadership, Kerrville became a center for wool storage, banking, and merchandising. Schreiner's brother-in-law, Caspar Real, was another leading sheep raiser in Kerr County.

Johanna Wilhelm was once known as the "Sheep Queen of West Texas" because she owned more sheep than any other woman in the state. At the turn of the century, her ranch covered more than a hundred sections in Menard and McCulloch Counties and was stocked with 10,000 to 15,000 sheep as well as large herds of cattle and goats. Hermann Stieler of Comfort and his sons became leading sheepmen in Kendall County about the same time. Adolf Stieler, one of the sons, later was known as the "Angora Goat King of the World."

Robert J. Kleberg Sr.

Captain Charles Schreiner

Again in 1917 war threatened to interrupt this peace and prosperity and to set Anglo-Americans against their neighbors of German descent. Germans were suspected once more of disloyalty. The use of the German language in public places and in schools was outlawed, and, in general, Germans were eyed with considerable distrust.

Were they disloyal? Almost without exception the Germans considered themselves loyal Americans ready to fight if necessary. Obviously, however, they still felt a natural sympathy with their ethnic homeland. Scattered copies of war novels like Hindenburg's *March into London* (Leipzig, 1915) can be found in some of the old libraries, but this is not necessarily an indication that German Texans secretly longed for a Central Powers victory over the Allies. More common in the lore of the Central Texas German belt is the type of story in which a wizened family patriarch warns his soldier sons and grandsons that this is a "new day," that they must not forget that they are "fighting under a new flag."

Although many Germans in Texas still maintained ties with their European kin, few found themselves in the mixed-up political situation of the von Donop family of Plehweville in Mason County. The three von Donop brothers in Texas still owned interests in their ancestral manor house in Lippe. In addition, the brothers had cousins who were general officers in the German, British, and French armies, which were at war.

In short, while many German Texans probably did feel considerable personal affinity with the German Empire in the early years of World War I, their patterns of political, economic, and social assimilation should leave no doubt that they were realistic and reasoned enough to know that, once the United States entered the war, it was a different situation.

A new generation had hardly grown up before the nation was once more at war with Germany in World War II. The use of German in public was again curtailed, but this time no one harbored serious doubts about the "loyalty" of the German Texans.

Many German-Texan soldiers and officers played important roles in the European theater because their fluency in German facilitated military operations. Descendants of German immigrants participated in the first Rhine crossing during the grim final months of World War II. German family names are found in nearly every roster of Texas's own 36th Infantry Division, which saw continuous action from the Allied invasion of Italy to the Normandy landing on D-Day 1944. During the occupation, when Sergeant Henry Kissinger was a military administrator in the Odenwald, several German Texans were active on the local level of the Allied occupation government of Germany. At least three German Texans rose to positions of great responsibility in the military during World War II. General Walter Krueger, a native of Germany and long-time military resident of San Antonio, had begun his career during the Spanish-American War. He was promoted to lieutenant general in 1941 as commander of the Third Army headquarters at Fort Sam Houston, where his chief of staff was a promising officer with an anglicized German surname—Eisenhower. At the request of General Douglas MacArthur, Krueger assumed command of the Sixth Army in the Pacific Theater, and by 1945 he had earned his fourth star.

After Pearl Harbor President Franklin Delano Roosevelt promoted a Texan of German ancestry to be commander of the Pacific Fleet. Chester Nimitz was born in Fredericksburg in a house still preserved on the main street. He was the grandson of Captain Charles

Cadet Chester W. Nimitz on leave from Annapolis

Nimitz, pioneer hotel owner and one-time boatman. The younger Nimitz grew up in Fredericksburg and Kerrville, going on to the United States Naval Academy as a cadet in 1901. He graduated from the

*Fleet Admiral Nimitz, one
of the few Americans, with
General Eisenhower, to hold
five-star rank*

Academy with distinction in 1905 and rose steadily in rank until President Roosevelt chose him over 28 senior flag officers to be Pacific Fleet Commander, one of the most difficult assignments of World War II. His combat assignment ended on the USS *Missouri*, when he accepted the Japanese surrender. Named Fleet Admiral in 1944, Nimitz later served as Chief of Naval Operations until his retirement in 1947. Since his death in 1966, the citizens of Fredericksburg have developed a museum on the site of his grandfather's famous hotel in his honor and for all who fought with him.

General of the Army Dwight D. Eisenhower led the Allied forces to victory in Europe. His German forebears from Heppenheim and the Odenwald immigrated to Pennsylvania a century before the German colonization in Texas began and eventually moved west to Kansas. Eisenhower's parents, like many impoverished German farmers from Kansas, were drawn to Texas in the late 1880's by the expansion of the railroads. They returned shortly after Eisenhower's birth in 1890 to Abilene, Kansas, where the future military leader and president grew up. His military career, however, got under way at Fort Sam Houston in the years before World War I. He was again stationed in

The Eisenhower family, with young Dwight standing in the center

San Antonio when he learned of his assignment to Europe in World War II. As Supreme Commander of Allied Expeditionary Forces during World War II, Army Chief of Staff after the war, president of Columbia University, Supreme Allied Commander in Europe to organize NATO forces, and President of the United States from 1952 to 1960, Eisenhower's life was one of great accomplishment.

Nearly 500,000 persons of at least one-half German descent were living in Texas in 1975. Excepting the large Anglo-American element in the population, German Texans are outnumbered only by black and Mexican Texans. In the military, in politics, medicine, engineering, science, manufacturing, business, banking, ranching, farming, and many other fields, German Texans have contributed substantially to the state's general prosperity. While melding into the general pattern of Texas life. their folklife retains in a number of regions the traditional German customs that recall a distant heritage. Their small towns and well-kept farmsteads, however, testify to their love of this land. They believed in this land and its future—fought for it, hallowed it with their labors, respected it—and it rewarded them abundantly.

GEORGE B. ERATH

*A*rriving in Texas in 1833, George B. Erath contributed substantially to the settlement of the western part of the state in a time when competent surveyors also had to be skillful Indian fighters. In 1835, serving with John H. Moore's Ranger force, he participated in a cavalry charge against a large band of Indians. The high-spirited mustang Erath was riding dashed far ahead of the advancing line. His efforts to restrain the animal were completely useless, and he was forever after dubbed "The Flying Dutchman."

He fought as a private at San Jacinto and later served in the congress of the Texas Republic; he also was a member of the first legislature after statehood. In 1849 he surveyed the town of Waco, where he made his home two years later. He also laid out the towns of Caldwell and Stephenville and made many surveys along the Brazos River.

George B. Erath died in 1891 in Waco. His memoirs, edited by his daughter and published in the *Southwestern Historical Quarterly*, provide a vivid picture of life in Texas during his first decade here. Erath County, which he explored and to which he led the first group of settlers, is named for this vigorous and wide-ranging Austrian immigrant.

Betty Holekamp

Caroline Grobe

Johanna Dorothea Charlotte Auguste
Wilhelmine Rosenberg Schelper

SIDESADDLE THROUGH TEXAS

Sometimes women had their own ideas about how the West should be won. The German-Texan women were often rather an unorthodox lot. As capable as their husbands, they rose to the demands of the frontier with grace, good humor, and a great deal of faith.

Mrs. Betty Holekamp grew up in the household of King Ernst August of Hanover. In 1844 she and her husband "set sail for Texas in the full glow of youth and hope," in the words of historian Guido E. Ransleben.

"They proceeded overland in the company of Prince Solms to the site chosen for New Braunfels. Arriving at the Guadalupe, they found this river in one of its periodic rises; however, Prince Solms, wishing to impress his companions with his daring and courage, plunged into the raging waters on his magnificent white horse. Not to be outdone, Mrs. Holekamp rode into the swollen waters and successfully crossed over, to the astonishment of the colonists."

Shortly thereafter, however, she fell from the prince's good graces. When Texas was admitted to the Union, Mrs. Holekamp gathered bits of colored cloth to make a United States flag, which was then unfurled on the public square. The prince, who had opposed annexation, was sorely offended by this disloyalty on the part of one of his "subjects."

Grossmutter (Grandmother) Caroline Grobe from Hanover came to Texas as a young girl because she was tired of the way she was being brought up! As soon as she landed, she found herself sick with malaria and all her worldly possessions—a chest of linens and other clothes—ruined by wet weather. She married the next year and moved with her husband and his children from two previous marriages to the Crabapple community north of Fredericksburg. Some years later her husband was killed by Indians while he was building a rock fence.

With eight children to rear, ages one to 14, Caroline Grobe proved her strength and the power of her will. She tended stock, tilled the soil, and set each of the children up in substantial homes. Grossmutter Caroline Grobe died at the age of 82, the matriarch of her persevering family.

Resolution and character line the face of the old woman who was one of the earliest Adelsverein settlers in Texas. Johanna Dorothea Charlotte Auguste Wilhelmine Rosenberg, from a Protestant merchant family in Göttingen, was the wife of New Braunfels's first brick-maker, Heinrich Lorenz Schelper. The story is often told of how she abducted her infant grandson from her Catholic daughter-in-law and presented him for baptism to the Protestant pastor of New Braunfels. The daughter-in-law responded with a firmness of her own and a fierce determination not to be outdone. Later on the same day she carried the child to the Catholic church for a second baptism.

Emma Murck Altgelt, who presided with great dignity and charm over the fashionable life of San Antonio's King William district, fell in love with Texas the very first time she heard of it. "It sounded like a fairy tale to me. The beautiful blue of the skies, the clear atmos-phere so peculiar to this country, the sun and its powerful rays charmed me. I roamed about and looked at the new countryside, the strange grasses, shrubs, and flowers. How I admired the many varieties of cacti and palms!"

Later she confessed to a secret joy. "I have always regarded looking for cows with their young calves as a pleasure. Besides a revolver, a coffee pot and provisions tied to the saddle were taken along and the saddle blanket was used for a camp bed. It is a pleasure to lie in the grass, to gaze at the blue heavens with bright stars, fall asleep, and wake up at the singing of the birds. There are, however, two sides to every story. Frequently the dew is so heavy that one is soaked and gets cold. Snakes like to crawl under the cover of the sleeper. Though not every one is a rattlesnake . . . the touch of any snake makes one shudder."

Emma Merck Altgelt

PROFESSOR BRODBECK
Inventor of a "Flying Machine"

Long before Luckenbach, Texas, reached its present-day promi-
nence as a country-music gathering place for city folk, its
local schoolmaster launched one of the world's first manned
flights. Jacob Brodbeck used every cent he earned teaching at Luckenbach to perfect his flying machine and apparently solved many of the
problems of manned flight long before the development of the inter-
nal combustion engine made modern aviation possible. Brodbeck
launched models of his flying machine at Fredericksburg and Luckenbach between 1846 and 1862. His experimental craft had a rudder,
wings, and a propeller and was powered by coiled springs.

In the summer of 1865, Jacob Brodbeck announced plans to
build and fly a full-scale "airship." He offered "certificates of interest"
to investors who would finance the trial flight. "The day for the great
trial test arrived, and the ship sailed away," wrote Fredericksburg historian Don Biggers in 1925. "Then the inventor discovered that a
spring will not wind up and down at the same time. He was several
feet higher than a tall tree when he made this discovery. The inventor
survived the crash, but the machine did not."

The episode completely scared off his backers. After several
years of touring the East in search of support, Jacob Brodbeck gave up
and returned to eke out an existence on his farm at Luckenbach. He
was unable to obtain a patent on his invention, but the Wright brothers' subsequent success in 1903 justified Brodbeck's confidence in the
feasibility of flight.

AUGUST C. BUCHEL
Brigadier General, C.S.A.

*T*he most spectacular soldier from the German settlements of Texas to serve in the Confederate army was Brigadier General August Carl Buchel, a small, quiet bachelor who spoke seven languages fluently. He may well have been the most noted soldier of fortune in all of Texas's history. Born in the state of Hesse in 1813, Buchel was trained in both German and French military schools. At 18 he was a second lieutenant in the Hesse-Darmstadt Volunteers. Five years later he was with the French army in Spain, where his conspicuous gallantry in the Carlist Wars earned him decorations and knighthood from Spanish Queen-Regent Maria Christina. Employed then as an instructor by the Ali Pasha, he rose to colonel in the Turkish army and was given the honorary title of pasha. Returning to Germany, he acquired a widespread reputation as a duelist which eventually forced him to emigrate.

In 1845 August Buchel sailed for Texas, landing at Indianola just before the outbreak of the Mexican War. He immediately organized a company of German immigrants to fight for the American cause. At the Battle of Buena Vista in Mexico, he was on the staff of General Zachary Taylor and won a commendation for bravery and Taylor's lasting admiration.

Buchel was serving as collector of customs at Port Lavaca in 1859 when the so-called "Cortina War" broke out on the Rio Grande border. He organized a company of Indianola volunteers and joined the fight. His company had barely been disbanded from this action when the Civil War began; he rose from lieutenant colonel to brigadier general before he was fatally wounded while leading a Confederate charge at the Battle of Pleasant Hill in April 1864. Buried near the battlefield, his body was later removed to Austin. His monument, recounting his amazing military record in six wars, is one of the most interesting in the Texas State Cemetery.

Herman Lehmann often donned his old "warpath" costume and feathered headdress for ceremonial occasions. He, along with two other captives, Clint and Jeff Smith, similarly abducted by Indians, was a popular attraction year after year at meetings of the Old Time Trail Drivers' Association in San Antonio.

LIFE WITH THE INDIANS
Voluntary and Involuntary

One of the most colorful immigrants was young Baron Emil Kriewitz from Prussia, who arrived in Texas in time to volunteer for the command of Captain August Buchel in the Mexican War. After his six-months' service expired, Kriewitz joined Meusebach in Fredericksburg. Here he accompanied the peace mission to the Comanches and remained for a while with the tribe as the Adelsverein's agent. Dressing like an Indian, the young soldier of fortune came to Fredericksburg with the tribe to ratify the 1847 peace treaty. The rumor was widely circulated that he married the daughter of Chief Buffalo Hump.

He later guided the Forty to Bettina on the Llano in 1847 and by 1852 was living at Castell, where he was a farmer, grocer, and postmaster. He served as county judge and justice of the peace of Llano County. Baron Kriewitz's experiences with the Indians became a highly embellished legend before his death at Castell in 1902.

Another legend in his own lifetime was Herman Lehmann, who spent eight years with Apache and Comanche Indians. He was captured as an 11-year-old at Loyal Valley northwest of Fredericksburg in 1870. By the time he was returned to white civilization in 1878, he had become a minor chief.

While he was with the Indians, Lehmann learned to love their free and colorful life. The chief taught him to ride wild horses and to jump from the ground onto a horse's back as it ran by, while dodging an arrow at the same time. He hunted buffalo and took part in Indian raids, covering wide expanses of the American Southwest. Later, when the tribe was captured and brought to Fort Sill, Lehmann became a good friend of Quanah Parker. Lehmann despised captivity at Fort Sill. "So that was the end of our Indian ways, our free, roving times which we loved. We were one of the very last tribes to come in." Finally Quanah Parker persuaded Lehmann to go back to his family in Texas.

After he returned to Loyal Valley, Lehmann eventually married a German girl and settled down to become proprietor of a country tavern and dance hall. Occasionally, over the years, Lehmann renewed his old Indian associations by traveling to Fort Sill, where he visited with Quanah Parker and other Indian chiefs. Herman Lehmann was doubtlessly one of the most colorful individuals in the Hill Country. Neighbors testified that "Herman can entertain a whole crowd with his Indian stories, and the beauty of it is, we believe them."

Prince Otto von Bismarck

"The Watch on the Rhine" took to the field—in Texas!

German Texans gloried in the success of Prince Otto von Bismarck, hero of the second German fatherland. The Prussian victory over the French at Sedan in 1870 and the unification of the German Empire in 1871 led to a cult of Bismarck hero worship throughout the United States. *Harper's Weekly* called him "Germany's most illustrious statesman."

The Bismarck Saloon in Fredericksburg was named for him, and in Comfort a German father named his newborn son after the battle at Sedan.

An American cavalryman stationed at a U.S. Army outpost in West Texas noted that the war between the Germans and the French continued in West Texas even after the peace treaty was signed in Europe. "During the summer and fall of 1870, the Franco-Prussian War being in progress, many scrimmages occurred between the German and French soldiers in the command, and although the French were few in numbers, they made up for it in an excess of patriotism. But the Germans had the best of it; the majority of the military band was from the fatherland, and the 'Wacht am Rhein' and other of their national airs were played morning, noon and night to the disgust of the 'enemy.' The Frenchmen would get together and sing the 'Marseillaise,' and occasionally blows were struck but not much damage was done, and finally the officers prohibited the playing of the aggravating tunes for the time being."

The Bismarck Saloon in Fredericksburg

Karl Wilhelm von Rosenberg

THE VON ROSENBERGS
A Family of Mapmakers

*T*hree generations of the von Rosenbergs had distinguished careers as mapmakers in Texas. Karl Wilhelm von Rosenberg, a licensed surveyor and architect, left Germany amid political and economic turmoil late in 1849. At the age of 28, he came with his entire family—wife, parents, and eight brothers and sisters—to Texas. They settled near Round Top in Fayette County. In 1856 he sold his farm there and moved to Austin, obtaining employment as a draftsman at the General Land Office. By 1861 he was chief draftsman. His career was interrupted by the Civil War, in which he served as a topographical engineer for the Confederacy. He returned to the Land Office until Reconstruction began, then opened a land agency of his own and prospered until his death in 1901.

His son, Ernst, became a draftsman in the General Land Office in 1876 and eventually rose to chief draftsman. Except for a two-year interval, he continued there until his death in 1915. Two of Ernst's sons, Herman and Ernest, were topographers with the old State Reclamation Department when that agency was consolidated with the General Land Office in 1939. Herman resigned because of ill health in 1952, and Ernest retired in 1954. When the Red River boundary dispute arose between Texas and Oklahoma in the 1920's, the von Rosenbergs and the Penick brothers did the topographical work for the state attorney general's office. Their work was so outstanding that both the state of Oklahoma and the federal government discarded their own maps and asked permission to use the Texas maps.

PHOTOGRAPHY

*T*he German Texans loved pictures. They had themselves photographed again and again throughout their lives. Babies, birthdays, parties, weddings, funerals, anniversaries, pets, homes, shops, gardens, cars, and dresses were thus preserved for all time in ambrotypes, tintypes, *cartes de visite*, and other paper photographs. Rare was the family parlor that did not have at least one rose or green plush-covered album in which row upon row of such pictures peered from their little openings in ornately decorated pages.

One inventive young German Texan helped the photographic industry in this country by popularizing what would become one of the standard parlor entertainments of the 1890's—stereopticon prints.

He almost lost his chance for fame, however, when he was captured during the Texas Revolution. William Langenheim, who had been in Texas since 1833, was 20 when he was taken prisoner by the Mexicans in the Battle of San Patricio in 1836. When he was released from a Mexican prison in 1837, Langenheim went to New Orleans and enlisted in the United States forces for the Seminole War. When his fighting days ended, he settled in Philadelphia and opened a photographic studio with his brother. They experimented with many of the new processes being developed for glass, metal, and paper photographs. The Langenheims introduced the stereographic process into the United States and were among the principal creators of the dual prints for viewers which soon graced practically every parlor table in the land.

Clara Moehring's early career hardly differed from that of any other turn-of-the-century photographer in Texas—except that she was a woman. The daughter of a gifted frontier photographer, she learned the refinements of her profession by helping in the studio. When her father died, Clara supported her mother and sisters. Her studio was based in Comfort, but a large part of her work came from a circuit she plied several times a year all over the Hill Country, like a traveling preacher. In the words of historian Margaret Kretzmeier, "Never was the weather too bad to photograph a home out in the country, even when the snow was ankle deep. Nor was it too much to arrange the folds of a bride's veil. She followed her father's footsteps in preserving a rich impression of local history."

Henry Jacob Braunig (1861-1945), prominent Texas photographer and businessman for 59 years, active in community and state affairs and development

A more recent German-Texan photographer achieved international fame. Eugene Omar Goldbeck crisscrossed the globe many times during a photographic career lasting more than 76 years. Goldbeck's first international recognition came from his 360° panoramic photography. As early as 1924, Goldbeck demonstrated his special talents of photographing battlefields, military ceremonies, naval formations at sea, and aerial views of volcanic eruptions. Shortly before World War II, Goldbeck had a serious argument with George Patton, but later the general "surrendered" to the photographer. Thereafter, Goldbeck was the only man in the world who had permission to photograph Patton's entire 14,000-man 2nd Armored Division.

He was an adventurous and tireless photographer. Today more than 60,000 negatives collected from Goldbeck's life work are preserved in the Harry Ransom Humanities Research Center of The University of Texas at Austin.

THE NEW LIFE
An Essay in Pictures

*The Great Barn on the ranch of Johanna Wilhelm (*above*) near Menard*

Now here I sat in the Texas hills listening to talk of cattle and weather and guns. We never spoke of labor unions. We had none. Or of racketeers. They were nowhere near us. Even income tax was not a subject to gripe about. There was a depression, and we didn't pay any. The really important gripe was about the commissioner who failed to work the roads.

Vera Flach

Tester bed, c. 1860, probably made by Johann Umland

All artisans and all men capable of working, who came on the same ship with us, found employment with good wages immediately. The rest all were taken in, and if they can adapt themselves, they will hardly have to work more than a month without wages.

Ida Kapp

Wardrobe made by cabinetmaker Johann Peter Tatsch

Threshing at Cypress Creek

German pioneers came from their crowded fatherland to live in freedom in the wide open spaces of Texas. The first thing they did was to buy *land, more land* and then *still more*. And they made it produce. Their sons and grandsons were taught never to sell the land, good times or bad. But never to sell. *Buy more.*

Vera Flach

Perseverance Mill at Comfort *by Hermann Lungkwitz*

111

C.H. Guenther's first mill on Live Oak Creek in Fredericksburg

Old sawmill at Industry

 Julius Henchling	 A.J. Schneider	 F.J. Lindheimer	 Conrad Meyer
 Caroline Grobe	 E. Kapp	 Heinrich Weber	 Friedrich Rust
 Aug. Bauer	 W.V. Hinüber	 E. Schwethelm	 Sophia Herbst
 Aug. Pfeiffer	 Carl Krueger	 John Hoerner	 Robt. Kleberg
 Wilhelm Traugott Schuchardt	 Mrs. Emma Murck Altgelt	 Friedrich Schaeferkoeter	 Peter Honighausen

Interior of Spoetzel Brewery, Shiner, 1909

Beer vat at the Peter Bros. Brewery, San Antonio

It is almost two years since I left the home of my parents for this glorious country. You know well that my expectations were not small; but, honestly, I must solemnly affirm that I have not been disappointed. In many instances my expectations have been far surpassed. Every hour and day that I live here, I learn to love my new home better.

Victor Bracht, 1847

Louis Ehlers Cigars, Shiner

Adverstisement for Kohlberg Bros. Cigars, El Paso

CHAPTER FOUR

"And do not fail to bring the complete works of Goethe."

*G*erman colonists in Texas knew how to amuse themselves by unpretentious means. Here they had little, but they learned to find pleasure in the small things of everyday life. Their language, the one thing above all else that tied them together and bound them to their past, became a real source of entertainment through word games, riddles, and lively wit. Folk songs and literary classics warmed the heart and gave dignity to life. Proverbs preserved the folk wisdom of the past, while schools and churches assured a succession of articulate and educated descendants. Music was one of their greatest amusements, and they gathered for dancing whenever the slightest excuse offered itself. Neighborhood picnics gave spice to even the plainest food. Wine and beer were never wanting, even if they were homemade. Long before life became easier for them, the colonists were trying to make it more beautiful.

So little of what they had owned in Europe could be brought with them, and they missed the things they had left behind. "Be sure to bring all the sheet music you can collect," wrote Caroline Louise Sacks von Roeder to her relatives in 1835. "My piano is in excellent condition, even after the rough handling on the voyage and roaming about here in search of our final location. And do not fail to bring the complete works of Goethe," she continued. "Day before yesterday, the third anniversary of the poet's death, we all assembled and read aloud many of his poems. Ludwig read the beautiful poem

117

'Warte nur, bald ruhest Du auch.' ('Wait awhile, you will soon rest also.') All of us wept. Robert Kleberg began to sob and went out under the trees." [52]

Looking back on those hard times, Ottilie Fuchs Goeth recalled more than 50 years later that even then they found time for the beauty of their culture. "Father's singing was a true gift of God. On the piano lay Mozart's *Don Juan* and *The Magic Flute,* Haydn's *Creation* and many other treasures of the German masters." [53] They combined their pleasures with more serious pursuits as well. "Occasionally we go to dances, and two months ago we had a troupe of actors in Fredericksburg. Things are developing here. Our schools are very good now. There are eight teachers and ten schoolhouses," [54] wrote Carl Hilmar Guenther.

Many of the German colonists were well educated. Within a year most German settlements had built both a church and a school because of their equal importance in preserving the traditions to which the colonists were accustomed. In this respect the early Germans in Texas were following a pattern much like the Puritans of New England, the French at Quebec, and the Spanish in Mexico and South America, all of whom recognized knowledge as the conveyer of civilization.

Despite how their fun-loving horseplay, drinking, and dancing at social gatherings might have appeared to some frontier Baptist and Methodist Americans, the Germans were basically a very religious people. Sunday was a joyful day. For most of them—Lutherans, Catholics, and German Methodists—the church was so much a part of everyday life that they tended to take it for granted. The ringing of church bells in the homeland called the German from his bed at dawn. The clock in the church tower struck out the hours of his daily work. At twilight the church bells sounded time for rest. During the night the clock punctuated the hours of his sleep. In the same way, the church calendar—Advent, Christmas, Lent, Easter, Pentecost— measured out his year through winter to spring, to summer and autumn, assuring him that there was a time for all man's labors, a time for sowing, a time for reaping, and a time for rest.

The observances of the church ritual marked the German's life from birth to death. Baptism gave the child a name and, in a sense, introduced that child to the community of man. The child was given godparents at baptism to ensure both spiritual and social welfare. If the parents died, the godparents took the orphan into their family, so that the child was not a burden on the community. Confirmation, generally at the age of 14, was a mark not only of religious responsibility but also of beginning adulthood. Childhood was over, schooling behind, and now the youngster was ready to learn a trade in preparation for standing on his own. Marriage, likewise, had religious and social implications. Finally, death and the funeral sealed the person's memory in the mind of the community and affirmed to the living that life was a continual cycle, an evolution, an accumulation of knowledge and experience. Each individual was a part of the fabric of humanity. This view of life carried over in the German's thinking to history. All history, to a German, was a continual process; civilizations and countries were born, died, and replaced by new life. Everything had a purpose as all mankind strived toward something better, toward the "good life."

Seeing things as they did, as part of a bigger design, it is not surprising that the German colonists brought so much of their culture with them. In the areas of Texas where Germans constituted the ethnic majority of the population, they retained that culture, modified in various ways, for a surprisingly long time. At the center of that culture, more often than not, were their schools and their local churches and congregations. From 1840 to 1844, the Reverend Louis C. Ervendberg and Dr. Johann Anton Fischer organized Protestant congregations in Industry, Cat Spring, Biegel, La Grange, and Columbus. Other parishes were established at Galveston and Frelsburg. A synodal meeting of German ministers in the Texas republic took place in 1841 at Industry to draw up a constitution for the regulation of these churches. The commissioners-general of the Adelsverein engaged Protestant pastors for both New Braunfels and Fredericksburg. Within a few years of the founding of these two towns, Catholic parishes were also established. The German Methodists organized in La Grange in 1847, in Fredericksburg in 1849, and in Yorktown at about the same time. Methodists were especially strong in the rural communities north and west of Fredericksburg. The Evangelical Lutherans, who drew their first minister from the missionary school at Chrischona, Switzerland, were instrumental in establishing early Lutheran missions in New Braunfels, Seguin, San Antonio, Castroville, and Quihi. By 1860 the Evangelical Lutherans had organized 37 congregations. The strongest German church in the east-central area was the Missouri Synod Lutheran. The churches followed the Germans from their original colonies to the cities, so that, by the end of the 1850's, San Antonio, Austin, Galveston, and Houston had German congregations. The first German parish in Dallas developed at Garland.

Early ministers made numerous contributions to the social welfare of the settlers. German ministers gave impetus to the Sunday school, or *Kindergottesdienst,* movement, which at that time was just being introduced in the United States, and also organized a number of church service guilds dedicated to the improvement of life in the frontier communities. The churches encouraged the growth of schools, and often the minister served as teacher.

One pioneer minister in particular, Louis C. Ervendberg, formulated two lofty educational projects for the church. In 1844 he successfully obtained a charter for the establishment of Hermann's University to give German instruction in liberal arts, medicine, theology, and law. The Congress of the Republic of Texas donated land for the university, but the Civil War doomed the project to failure, and no classes were ever held in Texas's German university. After the founding of New Braunfels in 1845, Ervendberg established the Western Texas Orphan Asylum at Neu Wied a few miles from New Braunfels on the Guadalupe. The orphanage, administered by Ervendberg and his wife, Maria Sophie Dorothea, née Münch, provided home and education for children whose parents had died at Indianola and on the way to New Braunfels.

Ervendberg's first church in New Braunfels served also as the colony's earliest school, with Hermann F. Seele as the schoolmaster, just as the first Fredericksburg school met in the old Vereinskirche in

St. Mary's Cathedral, Austin—The name of the parish, which dates from 1851, was originally St. Patrick's. In 1866, apparently because of a large influx of Germans, the name changed to St. Mary of the Immaculate Conception.

120

the middle of town, with Johann Leyendecker and Jacob Brodbeck as teachers. Later another school was organized with August Siemering as schoolmaster.

The close association of church and school was not at all uncommon, explained a Fayette County pioneer in 1850. "As for the education of our children," wrote Georg Carl Willrich, "that has until recently been a source of great anxiety and concern, but this, just within the past few days, has been removed. On the ninth of this month the settlement here organized a church school council. An Evangelical and Lutheran congregation, long in existence in Lexington, South Carolina, has recently decided to take an interest in their fellow believers scattered all over Texas. For this purpose, they have sent several young clergymen to Texas to begin establishing schools for the children." [55]

A large number of other German settlements also built schools on their own initiative, in the beginning without government support. Most Germans strongly favored compulsory attendance at public schools. Meusebach's record in promoting support in the state government for public education was impressive. Another early leader was Adolphus Fuchs, who in 1849 petitioned the state legislature for aid in maintaining a school. Fuchs, a former minister who taught school at Cat Spring, felt that public schools were "undeniably the best way to Americanize the German population of Texas and to make good citizens of them." Evidently a large number of Germans agreed with him and Meusebach in this regard. Many years passed, though, before free public schools became widespread in Texas.

As the economic prosperity of the German Texans improved, private schools like the German-English School in San Antonio were established in many of the cities with significant German populations. Drawing enrollment from distant parts of the state, the nonsectarian German-English School at San Antonio ranked among outstanding educational institutions of 19th century Texas. In March 1858 this private school was organized with two inviolable principles followed throughout its 40-year life: religious instruction was prohibited, and German and English were required. The curriculum also included Spanish, geography, writing, poetry, history, algebra, arithmetic, sewing, and singing. Classes were moved from rented quarters in 1860 to a new stone structure on South Alamo Street. A prestigious German social club, the Casino Club, aided building funds with a centennial celebration commemorating the poet Friedrich von Schiller, to whom the school was dedicated. In 1870 a new two-story unit was dedicated to Baron Alexander von Humboldt, and still later two other additions

Julius Berends,
a refugee from revolution
in Germany and director of the
German-English School

The German-English School at San Antonio

were made. With development of free public schools, the German-English School closed sometime before 1897.

The development of German schools kept alive a fondness for German literature and thought among the younger generation of colonists. Louise Romberg Fuchs recalled, "Poems gave me great pleasure, and I liked to memorize them and later recite them at my work in the field, so that I would not forget them. For me it was a pleasure to rejoice in their beauty while I was working." [56] They still read, and they still studied, even after the Civil War broke out. "The harbors were blocked, nothing was coming in, not even newspapers. One turned again to the classics—Goethe, Lessing, Schiller, Shakespeare, as well as Jean Paul. People borrowed literature from one another. The German families traded books. What the one did not have, the other probably had." [57] Already before the war, such sharing of music and books had characterized life among the settlers. The pleasure derived from literature led to the organization of several small literary societies like the Prairieblume for young members of the Black Jack Creek community in Fayette County and later, the Damen Lese-Verein on Cypress Creek in Kerr County. Members of these literary societies met frequently at regular intervals to read German prose and poetry, to discuss their own writings, and sometimes to enact light theatrical performances.

Johannes Romberg, founder of the Prairieblume, was the foremost poet of the pioneer German Texans. A complete individualist and a passionate defender of personal liberty, Romberg expressed in his poetry no note of nostalgia or homesickness for the Germany he left behind; rather, he lived completely in the present, filled with a determination to overcome anything that blocked his family's happiness, and he lost no time in "planting both feet in Texas soil." [58] His Texas poetry is sometimes irreligious and antagonistic toward the church. Although Romberg's father, a minister, had wanted him to study theology, the boy's poor eyesight prevented his entering a university, and his parents decided instead to train him to become a businessman. Romberg, however, preferred carpentry and cabinetmaking, two occupations his family considered below their social standing, but his love for woodworking stood him in good stead in the New World, where he built two homes for his family. His great intelligence and cultural background, which in the Old World had kept him from the work he loved, enabled him here in Texas to educate his nine children and to teach them to value their freedom to enjoy the kind of life they wanted, free from the artificial social constraints which had handicapped him in his youth.

The family of Pastor Adolphus Fuchs was closely related by marriage to the Romberg family. Fuchs had been a Protestant minister in Germany until 1845 when he brought his family to Texas to give them the religious and social opportunities which life denied them in Europe. He had studied at Jena and Göttingen, and he knew French, Latin, Hebrew, Greek, and English in addition to German. Furthermore, he was an accomplished violinist, pianist, and singer, who wrote poems and set them to music as he did poems by Goethe, Schiller, Balzer, and others. These were compiled into a songbook after his death. Fuchs rarely served as a pastor in Texas, and then only sporadically, for he had become disillusioned with his calling. He taught school at Cat Spring and later taught music at Baylor College in Independence. His literary activity included translations into English of Hoffmann von Fallersleben's rousing Texas songs. In fact, von Fallersleben's song, "The Star of Texas," was written as a farewell tribute to Pastor Fuchs.

Professor Carl Herbst

Pastor Adolphus Fuchs

124

Many of the German-Texan writers were journalists. Carl Herbst, the schoolmaster at Comfort, put out a handwritten newspaper which circulated from subscriber to subscriber. Called *Der Bettelsack* (The Beggar's Bag), the paper was barely a step above the town crier in the development of journalism on the frontier. Fritz Goldbeck employed what he called light "prose verse" and contributed poems to this handwritten newspaper celebrating the beauty of Texas—its hills, trees, flowers, and streams. Like Romberg, Fritz Goldbeck delighted in the present, but his poetry is not deep.

A later Comfort poet, Ferdinand Lohmann, represented a different outlook on life. Lohmann wrote more about the past than about the present and in his poems lamented the gradual loss of German language, customs, and values which came as German Texans assimilated into the mainstream of American life. For Lohmann the price of success was too high; the Germans, according to him, gave up their most intimate possession, their mother tongue. He was a successful teacher, however, and he published books on teaching methods, in addition to several volumes of poetry.

August Siemering

Contrasting with Herbst's primitive journalism were the more advanced Galveston *Zeitung* (1846), Ferdinand Lindheimer's *Neu-Braunfelser Zeitung* (1852), Dr. Adolf Douai's radical abolitionist *San Antonio Deutsche Zeitung* (1853), and Gustav Schleicher's *San Antonio Staats-Zeitung* (1856). At least five other newspapers in Victoria and Galveston joined these papers before the beginning of the Civil War interrupted the expanding field of German journalism in Texas. After the war August Siemering, a moderate Sisterdale Forty-Eighter and former schoolteacher in Fredericksburg, began publication of the *Freie Presse für Texas* in San Antonio. Eighteen German newspapers were in existence by 1892, and the number peaked with 29 in 1907. Eleven papers ceased publication during World War I. When the United States entered World War II, Texas still had six German papers; by the end of the war, four were left, and the last of these, *Neu-Braunfelser Zeitung,* ceased publication in German in the 1950's.

Many pioneer German-Texan writers were closely associated with the church, the movement for public education, or the German-language press. Their poetry, memoirs, sketches, essays, and novels make up a valuable part of the cultural-historical literature of the Southwest. Some of the recurring characters in these writings are historical personages, Indians, explorers, hunters, ranchers, swindlers, gullible city-slickers, and incompetent immigrants.

Quite humorous is the conflict-of-nationalities theme, which—along with nostalgia, patriotism, social protest, and landscape description—often characterizes this literature. Like much local color and children's literature, these writings record the social conditions of Texas from before the republic until after the Civil War.

The early influx of well-educated professional Germans into the Texas lifestream made a marked impact also in such artistic fields as painting, lithography, sculpture, theater, and music. Two competent painters who came with the immigrants were Hermann Lungkwitz and Richard Petri. They were brothers-in-law who settled near Fredericksburg in 1851. Working there and in New Braunfels, they left sensitive paintings of Texas scenes and of the Indians they encountered on the frontier. Later Lungkwitz operated a photographic studio in San Antonio with artist Carl von Iwonski until 1870, then became a photographer for the General Land Office in Austin, but he continued landscape painting, mainly of the Texas Hill Country, until his death in 1891.

Carl G. von Iwonski came to Texas from Silesia as a youngster. His parents maintained a farm near New Braunfels, and here

Richard Petri, from a self-portrait (c. 1852)

Hermann Lungkwitz, artist and photographer

127

Carl Von Iwonski, portrait artist, teacher, and photographer

Artist Louise Wueste, from a photograph by Lungkwitz

young Iwonski taught himself to draw and paint while helping his father clear fields and build fences. His early drawings and watercolor paintings of the New Braunfels Dramatic Society preserve much of the cultural richness of the German amateur theater in Texas. In 1858 Iwonski moved to San Antonio, where he listed himself as a "painter" in the 1860 Bexar County census. Like other artists in the city, he supplemented his livelihood as a Biedermeier genre and portrait artist by teaching at the German-English school and by learning photography as well as by drawing fierce political cartoons after the war. When Reconstruction drew to a close, Iwonski felt compelled to leave Texas because his radical Republican activities made him unpopular. He died in 1912 in Breslau, Germany.

Another, less political, artist was Louise Heuser Wueste, talented daughter of a prosperous German family, who studied art under Karl Ferdinand Sohn at the Düsseldorf Academy. Widowed at an early age, she came to Texas in 1857 to live with her three married children, who had migrated earlier, and, in San Antonio during the Civil War, she taught drawing and painting. She was the most famous woman to enter this field dominated by other Germans—Petri, Lungkwitz, and Iwonski—and the French painter Theodore Gentilz. After the Civil War, Louise Wueste lived in Eagle Pass with her son until her death in 1875.

One of the most effective catalysts for the cultural ferment appeared on the scene in 1872 when the German sculptor Elisabet

Elisabet Ney in her Austin studio

Ney and her Scottish husband, Dr. Edmund Montgomery, bought a plantation near the town of Hempstead. Miss Ney was already famous in Europe with busts of Humboldt, Liebig, Kaiser Wilhelm I, Ludwig II, Garibaldi, and Schopenhauer to her credit, when she was commissioned by the state to make statues of Stephen F. Austin and Sam Houston for the Texas exhibit at the World's Fair in 1893. She built a studio called Formosa in Austin and eventually produced the two statues. Both are now in the rotunda of the Texas Capitol in Austin. She also sculpted a full-length, reclining figure of General Albert Sydney Johnston, which is mounted over the hero's grave in the Texas State Cemetery. Formosa has been preserved as a museum by the Texas Fine Arts Association.

Art, newspapers, literature, and literary societies, schools, and churches served to refresh the German's sense of cultural identity. This function extended also to theater, music and singing societies, casino clubs, and athletic associations. Still later, in the 20th century, as even these organizations declined in importance, the German-Texan immigrant ethnic museums afforded him an insight into his heritage.

The German penchant for coming together in societies and clubs, or *vereine*, was not a characteristic of the ethnic group alone but was also a response to being a minority in a predominantly Anglo-American culture. Most immigrant nationalities in America have gone through similar patterns.

The early literary societies, such as Romberg's Prairieblume, occasionally sponsored light theatrical performances. The early German theater in Texas really got under way, however, with the organization of the New Braunfels Dramatic Society in 1854. This amateur theater group owed its origin not only to the settlers' love of German drama but also to a very practical need in the town. New Braunfels needed a new school building, and the first six performances of the dramatic society raised money for a building fund. In the December 8, 1854, issue of the *Neu-Braunfelser Zeitung,* editor Lindheimer encouraged townspeople to turn out for these six plays. "This theater is a much more noble entertainment than to admire tightrope walkers, circus riders, clowns, black jesters, shadowplay, and other phantasmagories, which in the past year have carried well over $500 out of our city, a sum which we now could very well use for the building of our schoolhouse." [59]

The plays performed by the New Braunfels Dramatic Society included Schiller's *Kabale und Liebe,* Mendelssohn's *Er muss aufs land,* and Töpfer's *Rosenmüller und Finke oder Abgemacht.* For less practical purposes, theatrical performances were also undertaken in the early years by the social clubs of San Antonio, Galveston, and La Grange.

Casino Hall Dramatic Society, watercolor by Iwonski

In 1869 a theater opened under the direction of a German named Henry Greenwall in Galveston, and, for the next 40 years, he was a leading figure in Texas theatrical circles, with productions opening in Galveston, Houston, Dallas, Fort Worth, and Waco. Greenwall brought hits of the American and British stages as well as the classical German repertoire to Texas audiences. Austin's *Wochenblatt* also reported a lively German theater in the city. In 1879 it produced Gilbert and Sullivan's *H.M.S. Pinafore* and Balfe's *La Bohème* in English.

Singing societies have survived much longer than the theater groups, partly because they appeal to more people as social entertainment and partly because they do not require stages and equipment. Singing groups were formed in nearly every German settlement. Anyone familiar with songs from the homeland who enjoyed singing has always been welcome, so the membership of the singing societies even today is large. As one German historian explained, "The German immigrants who came to Texas brought along an invisible passenger, the German song. It accompanied them westward on their dreary march across the broad prairies and established itself on the beautiful banks of the Comal and Pedernales, to cheer them in their daily toil and brighten their evenings at the fireside." [60]

The first singing society, the Germania, was organized in New Braunfels in 1850 on the anniversary of Texas independence. Two years later the Germans held a special Fourth of July program and gave a concert to raise money for the purchase of a printing press. In the autumn of 1853, the first *Staats-Sängerfest* (state singers' festival) met in New Braunfels with singing clubs from New Braunfels, Sisterdale, Austin, and San Antonio in attendance. This was the beginning of an annual tradition which is still observed

The second *Staats-Sängerfest* took place in 1854 in San Antonio with the singing societies of New Braunfels, Sisterdale, San Antonio, Austin, and La Grange. The meeting assembled under the shadow of dark political overtones; it was used by some of the leaders to register German political consensus and social protest against slavery. At the same meeting, less ominous plans were laid toward the organization of the Deutsch Texanischer Sängerbund (German-Texan Singers' League).

"Even in my youth, when Texas was young too," wrote Emma Murck Altgelt, describing the third *Staats-Sängerfest* in 1855, "it had German singing societies. A music festival was held in New Braunfels. Many singers came from far away, among them a jolly group from Sisterdale. . . . They came by oxcart because, the day before, Indians had stolen all of the horses in the settlement. The suits of most of the

Beethoven Männerchor, 1893

men were quaint. Although they were aristocrats, not every one of them had a coat. The German apparel was worn out—little of it was new and that which was bought was inferior. A large singers' hall had been erected. The ladies furnished the flowers and wreaths. Everyone brought good humor, and many. . .songs were beautifully sung." [61]

Another reason for the popularity of these singing societies was recounted in a letter of 1856 from Fredericksburg. "This year at Pentecost we will have a big singing festival in Fredericksburg and in the evening a dance where I, as an eligible bachelor, must of course not be missing." [62]

After the Civil War, the singing clubs continued the state song festivals in San Antonio, New Braunfels, Fredericksburg, and other cities and towns. With the founding in 1867 of the Beethoven Männerchor under the direction of Mayor Wilhelm C.A. Thielepape, German singing in Texas entered a new era. This large men's choir met in the San Antonio Casino Hall until an imposing, two-story edifice was dedicated in 1895.

A three-day festival of Spring was celebrated with parades, pageants, and dances in 1876 to commemorate the centennial anniversary of the United States. Five years later a Hill Country league, the Texanischer Gebirgs-Sängerbund, was formed in Boerne. Also in 1881 the 13th state song festival assembled in Galveston. A 6,000-seat pavilion was erected on the beach for the spectacular event. All the German clubs gathered in Austin in 1888 to participate in the dedication of the new Capitol.

"Of all the festivals during the years that followed," in the words of Martha and Earl Fornell, "the 29th *Sängerfest,* held at Houston in 1913 to celebrate the diamond jubilee of the state *Sängerbund,* was probably the most dazzling. The mass chorus representing 21 German singing societies of Texas was assisted by two choruses of Houston schoolchildren—one numbering 300 and another 5,000—which sang during the matinee. The St. Louis Symphony Orchestra accompanied the mass chorus, and such outstanding performers as Carl Schlegel, baritone of the Berlin and New York operas, and Mme. Marie Rappold, soprano of the Metropolitan Opera Company of New York, sang on the program, which consisted almost entirely of works by German-American composers. Two numbers were by German Texans, Dr. Hans Harthan of Austin and Professor Frank Renard of Sherman." [63]

Neither of the World Wars stopped the songfests. By the time of the American bicentennial in 1976, both Texas singing leagues looked back on a rich tradition of German song in Texas. When a bicentennial observance to honor German pioneers was sponsored by the Volksfest Association of Texas in 1976, both singing leagues

Beethoven Männerchor, 1916. In the center of the composite is a photograph of the Beethoven Hall dedicated in 1895.

contributed to the festival program in San Antonio. Celebrating its 122nd anniversary, the Deutsch Texanischer Sängerbund consisted of nine member organizations: the Austin Sängerrunde (1879), Austin Sängerrunde Damenchor (1859), Beethoven Damenchor (1932), Beethoven Männerchor (1876), Dallas Frohsinn (1877), Houston Liederkranz (1925), Houston Sängerrunde (1883), Houston Sängerbund Damenchor (1938), and the San Antonio Liederkranz (1892). The Texanischer Gebirgs-Sängerbund still had eight member organizations, where its size had remained for nearly a century: the Arion Männerchor (1908), Beethoven Damenchor (1932), Beethoven Männerchor (1867), Boerne Choral Club (1924), Gesangverein Echo from New Braunfels (1894), Gemischter Chor Frohsinn from Clear Springs (1916), Gemischter Chor Harmonie from New Braunfels (1937), and the Hermannssöhne Gemischter Chor of San Antonio (1920).

The songs of that bicentennial program combined old German and new American selections. The German-Texan sense of ethnicity had evolved by 1976 into a curious, inward-looking mixture of two different cultures, political outlooks, and ways of life. The mixture was distinctive, like the appearance of the German-Texan towns. This sense of ethnic identity was their unique creation, something personal and vital. Most of them saw no contradiction in being both German and American at the same time. Perhaps most telling of their individual outlook is the German translation of the Preamble of the Constitution which prefaced the program of the Bicentennial Volksfest (which itself was printed in German with an English title on the cover).

Wir, das Volk	We, the people
der Vereinigten Staaten,	of the United States,
um eine vollkommene	in order to form
Vereinigung herbeizuführen,	a more perfect union,
Gerechtigkeit festzustellen,	establish justice,
innere Ruhe zu sichern,	ensure domestic tranquility,
für allgemeine Wohlfahrt	provide for
zu fördern	the common defense,
und den Segen der Freiheit	promote the general welfare,
für uns und	and secure the blessings
unsere Nachkommen	of liberty for ourselves
zu erhalten,	and our posterity,
beschliessen und verfügen	do ordain and establish
diese Verfassung	this Constitution
für die Vereinigten Staaten	for the United States
von Amerika.	of America.

FREETHINKERS IN THE HILL COUNTRY

*T*he striking exception among the German Texans with regard to religion is the town of Comfort. With its Bettina and Sisterdale "Latin Colony" antecedents, the town had developed somewhat differently than the Adelsverein colonies of New Braunfels and Fredericksburg.

Comfort, Sisterdale, and San Antonio were centers of radical political ideas during the Civil War. This same liberal-thinking element also revolted against established religion.

"Nearly all German-Americans in Comfort were freethinkers, as were their brilliant ancestors in the Latin Colony. Those pioneers said frankly that they left Germany to escape not only political persecution but also religious oppression. They wished to be free on all counts. From 1849 to 1892, 43 years, no church was built in our community. In very few of the homes was there a Bible or any religious literature. There were no prayers. At funerals sentimental German ballads were sung. I never heard Luther's great ode to Belief: 'A mighty fortress is our God, a bulwark never failing.' The attitude toward organized religion ran the gamut from mild anticlericalism to bitter denunciation.

"When occasionally a minister conducted a funeral and asked for the Lord's Prayer, they . . . did not know it.

"Funerals were always large as they would be with so many relatives near at hand. The service was conducted by a German lodge and its message was 'Rest in Peace.' The life of the deceased was told and sometimes there was a eulogy read by a man skilled in public speaking. There was no mention of immortality because no one believed in it. We live in our children. That is our only immortality."

Observations of Vera Flach in
A Yankee in German America

GEORGE PFEUFFER

George Pfeuffer was active in political life for less than a decade, but he devotedly and effectively served the cause of public education in that time. Born in 1830, he was a native Bavarian, who landed with his family at Galveston when he was 15. The family took passage to Indianola and lost their belongings in a shipwreck on the final leg of their voyage.

They made their way to New Braunfels, and young Pfeuffer became a clerk in John F. Torrey's store. In 1846 the lad went to Corpus Christi, where he later became secretary to H.L. Kinney. Pfeuffer returned to New Braunfels in 1861 and began working for a San Antonio-based firm. After the war he and his brother organized their own firm in New Braunfels.

In 1877 Pfeuffer served as Comal County judge. Three years later Governor Oran M. Roberts appointed him as head of Texas A&M College. In 1882 Pfeuffer was elected to the state senate, where he continued to support the college's interests as chairman of the education committee. He became chairman of A&M's governing board in 1884 and led a fight to provide a permanent state endowment for the institution. His practice of strict economy in food purchases for the college produced a large surplus of funds with which a dormitory, Pfeuffer Hall, was built after his death in 1886.

A TEACHER REMINISCES

Schoolmaster Hubert Heinen, a descendant of pioneer ranching families of the Hill Country, taught for nearly 40 years in Comfort. When he began teaching, the school had three rooms and three teachers. At the end of his long career, his relatives and the townspeople encouraged him to write an autobiography. He began with an account of his own school years in the 1880's.

"At that time the Comfort School was on the block now known as the park. The grounds were equipped with a gymnastics pole—*Turnstange*—a double bar and a long smooth ladder, which were used for gymnastic purposes. A regular period of instruction in these gymnastics was set aside every Friday afternoon. The girls, of course, did not perform, but I recall at one time they were given instruction in marching and drills.

"The old school bell was in a steepled tower on the roof. Two ropes hung down to be used by the teacher *only* for ringing that old school bell—20 or 30 peals before opening school and again at the close of classes.

"Each teacher took care of two grades: the first and second in one room, the third and fourth in the other. There were no written tests, but a good deal of written work was done and preserved, with corrections, in copy books. One half of the lessons were supposed to be in English, the other half in German. Since German was . . . spoken on the school grounds and in the homes, it is understandable that very little English was learned.

"Children were . . . eight, often nine, years old before entering school. The school year lasted ten calendar months, . . . the vacation was timed so the children could help picking cotton.

"There were regular readers. German was easy, but English was naturally difficult. To an Anglo-American our pronunciation and 'butchering up' of the English language no doubt would have been both amusing and horrifying. The few English-speaking pupils had no choice but to learn to speak German on the playground.

"A reading lesson was assigned each day. We were told to read this lesson over three times in preparation for the following day. Each pupil was called on to read one sentence aloud, standing up, in regular order as we were seated. This gave us—me included—an opportunity to figure out beforehand which sentence we were to read, hurriedly read it over several times before our time came, thus evading our homework. That explains, my dear former pupils, why you never could tell when your turn came to read!

"Regular hours were provided for penmanship practice, and every child learned to write legibly. The English letters were known as Roman.

"Besides penmanship exercises, we wrote essays or stories and translations.

"The four fundamentals of arithmetic—addition, subtraction, multiplication, and possibly division—were taught the first year. Multiplication tables to 12 inclusive had to be mastered . . . all had learned to count—at least in German—up to 100 before entering school.

"Other subjects were English and German grammar, geography, declamation, singing, and gymnastics.

"Playthings for children were unknown. To cart away rocks lying loose about the house, father fixed up a cart with wooden wheels and a long pole. Crude as it was, this contraption afforded more pleasure perhaps than many youngsters nowadays get from more modern conveyances.

"Corncobs, potatoes with sticks in them for legs and horns, served as animals. These—the cobs—I branded with a branding iron in the shape of a plow.

"For other pastimes we had established several playgrounds under shady trees at different points. One was 'Comfort,' another 'San Antonio,' and just beyond 'San Antonio' was 'Deutschland,' showing how extensive was our knowledge about the universe!"

FRITZ GOLDBECK
Comfort's Early Poet

*F*ritz Goldbeck's love of life's simple joys is expressed in an oft-told story about him and his brother, Theodore, related here by Robert Robinson-Zwahr. "During their sojourn in Comfort, the Goldbeck brothers were responsible on one occasion for the Fourth of July celebration taking place a day early. Confronted with the delivery of several kegs of beer (from San Antonio's Menger Brewery) which would spoil if not drunk quickly, they fired the cannon reserved to call residents together in case of an Indian attack or another emergency. The people who quickly responded soon lost their indignation at the ruse and began the annual celebration a day before schedule."

DR. ADOLF DOUAI

*T*he descendant of a family of French refugees in Germany, Dr. Adolf Douai was forced by poverty to give up his university studies and to take a position as a tutor in Russia, where he eventually obtained his doctorate. He returned to Germany in time to participate in the civil unrest leading to the 1848 Revolution. Douai and his wife, Baroness von Beust, felt they had no choice then but to leave Europe. Called the first popularizer of Marxian ideas in the United States, Douai's outspokenness resulted in his near ruin on several occasions. Driven from New Braunfels, where he had taught, he became the editor of the *San Antonio Deutsche Zeitung,* in which he advocated the abolition of slavery. When he was drummed out of the state in 1856, he went to Boston. His first school there was destroyed after an allegedly atheistic commemoration of Humboldt. He survived, however, to become known for his introduction of the kindergarten system in the United States.

SELMA METZENTHIN-RAUNICK

S elma Metzenthin-Raunick, born in Berlin, was a descendant of aristocratic German families. Educated mostly in Texas and Pennsylvania, she became the historian of the German writers in Texas. Her numerous articles were published in the United States and Germany, and she also lectured in both countries.

A poet herself, Metzenthin-Raunick wrote *Verses from an Invalid's Pen* (1923), two volumes of *Deutsche Schriften in Texas* (1931 and 1934), and *Rise Up, O World* (1944). Her prose writings recall a child's perception of family life in her new world.

"This Texas—they loved it. They could talk and play and sing as much as they pleased, and their parents, whom they had hardly seen in the old home, played with them. Why, it all seemed too good to be true. Father and mother taught them now, and their teaching was different from that of governess and preceptress. And father and mother worked with them and laughed while they worked. The parents did not look pompous or dignified any longer. They had packed away their elaborate and costly clothing, and mother had made some plain dresses for herself and the children. Only on holidays she got out their finery and then selected the simplest she could find. The governess had never tolerated the slightest spot on the children's clothing, and they must always have clean hands and wear gloves. Their mother had taught them the use of soap and water to clean clothing as well as soiled hands. And as for gloves—they were never worn.

"It was not quite so easy for the parents to adapt themselves to the new conditions. True, they also breathed more freely, moved more freely than in the narrow aristocratic circles abroad, but they were too deeply rooted in the old customs, too closely connected with their people in the fatherland not to feel, occasionally, a pang of longing, a touch of regret. But on the whole they were happy, for the first time in their life genuinely and unrestrainedly free and happy with their children."

EDNA BIERSCHWALE
American Impressionist

A descendant of four pioneer families of the Hill Country, the German-Texan artist Edna Bierschwale was born in 1907 in Comfort. Her parents sent her to Sophie Newcomb College in New Orleans, and, when she later returned to Texas, she studied art with José Arpa, Xavier Gonzales, and Etienne Ret in San Antonio. She painted predominantly in watercolors in the impressionistic manner.

Edna Bierschwale by Xavier Gonzales

"BUCK" SCHIWETZ

*I*hope to leave behind me a collection of indigenous paintings which will faithfully portray Texas as it is," says E.M. "Buck" Schiwetz, one of the state's favorite landscape artists. Born at Cuero in 1898, he painted an exceptionally fine watercolor—an old cabin in a woodland—when he was 12. Encouraged by his artistic mother, he developed considerable painting proficiency before going to Texas A&M College, where he majored in architecture. After brief periods in Dallas, Houston, and New York, Schiwetz settled permanently in Houston in 1929 and became the artist member of an advertising partnership but continued to sketch and record Texas scenes and Texas architecture through the 1970's.

The Ottomar von Behr House in Sisterdale by "Buck" Schiwetz

OSCAR FOX

*O*scar Fox was the first Texas-born composer to achieve wide fame. Born in 1879, he was a grandson of Adolph Fuchs, the minister, farmer, and educator who had once taught music at Baylor College in Independence. Educated in San Antonio and Zurich, Switzerland, Oscar Fox was an organist, choirmaster, and teacher in various Texas cities before winning national recognition with his musical settings of cowboy songs collected by John Lomax. Fox continued to compose music from 1922 until his death in 1961. Lyrics for "The Hills of Home," his best-known composition, were written by Floride Calhoun, who was living at that time in San Antonio. She was referring to the hills of New York State, but, when Fox set the poem to music, *he* was thinking of Burnet County, Texas, where he was born.

WILHELM C.A. THIELEPAPE

*B*orn in Illinois in 1814, Wilhelm C.A. Thielepape became a leader of San Antonio's political and cultural life. He was an architect by profession, but his great loves in life were painting and singing—he was an accomplished portrait artist, and he had a fine singing voice. Under his leadership, the Beethoven Männerchor was organized. Because he was a German and a Republican, Thielepape was appointed mayor of San Antonio by General J.J. Reynolds and Governor E.J. Davis and held that office from 1867 until 1872. After the end of Reconstruction, he moved to Chicago.

DR. RUDOLPH L. BIESELE
Historian of the German Texans

*P*ublished in 1931, Biesele's *The History of the German Settlements in Texas* remains the basic work on Texas immigration history. Biesele's father, Leopold, came to Guadalupe County in 1851 after fighting in the revolution of 1848. He earned a living as a farmer and as a teacher. His son, Rudolph, was born in 1886 and attended his father's school on York Creek, then graduated from Seguin High School. He entered college at Southwest Texas State Normal School in San Marcos but graduated from the University of Texas at Austin in 1909. In 1910 he married Anna Emma Jahn, granddaughter of the New Braunfels cabinetmaker Johann Michael Jahn. He received his doctorate in history from the University of Texas in 1928. Biesele taught in public schools at New Braunfels, Corsicana, and Waco. Later he joined the faculty at the University of Alabama, taught briefly at Louisiana Polytechnic Institute, then came back in 1931 to the University of Texas, where he remained until retirement.

146

The Steves Homestead

KING WILLIAM STREET
An Essay in Pictures

The first house on King William Street was built in 1867 by Ernst Altgelt, who gave the street its name. Altgelt helped develop the area into the first prominent residential section of San Antonio. Architects created elegant homes in this 35-block neighborhood to reflect the great wealth and refined taste of the city's new elite.

The industrial revolution had brought new wealth to some families. The King William district exemplifies this age when people took to conspicuous consumption—in buildings, clothes, fixtures, and furnishings. These elaborate possessions required more work than their simpler predecessors, but now servants were available. Men made the fortunes, but the coming of leisure ushered in a woman's world. The influence of women extended outside the home directly and indirectly into politics, church, business, and society.

Portrait of Edward Steves
by Carl G. von Iwonski

Carl Hilmar Guenther

148

Carl Groos Residence, 1900

Parlor in Carl Hilmar Guenther's house, 1902

The founder of a successful manufacturing enterprise in Texas, Edward Steves came in 1848 with his father and settled in New Braunfels. In 1855 he was a pioneer settler on Cypress Creek west of the new town of Comfort, where he farmed and did carpentry. During the Civil War, his brother and brother-in-law were among those massacred by Confederate troops at the Battle of the Nueces while trying to escape to Mexico. After the war Steves moved to San Antonio and built a successful lumber, sash, and door business which eventually expanded to Corpus Christi, Victoria, and San Angelo. His Victorian mansion on San Antonio's prestigious King William Street became a San Antonio showplace, a residence which captured the spirit of an age and a place.

Staircase, Steves Homestead

Anton Wulff garden, 1892

Garden party at the Anton Wulff house, 1892

CHAPTER FIVE

"This culture is nearly at an end."

o a German Texan growing up a century after troubles in the fatherland had sent scores of idealists to these shores, the Germans' early years in Texas held a rich tradition of cultural diversity. It was a time when the two cultures—the German and the American—were equal, existing side by side but not yet feeling self-conscious. The lifestyle was no longer that which the immigrants had brought over. German culture had been transformed somehow as it took root in Texas soil.

The old ones still remembered a different time. As Vera Flach noted in the 1960's, "Now that this culture is nearly at an end, one looks at the older generation, still speaking the beloved language, maintaining their identity, preserving their antiques in museums, reading yellowed letters and diaries; and one speculates about them." [64] Many regretted the blending of the old ways with the American way of life, yet they realized that this mixing was inevitable and that their children were heirs of two spirits. Much had been lost from the German tradition, but a good part of that heritage was strong. A part which was fun-loving and colorful had taken on its own character in the Texas hills and prairies.

"Whatever their reasons for coming and whatever attitudes they had about their mother country, they were still Germans when they got here," wrote Texas folklorist Francis E. Abernethy. "The songs they sang, the stories they told and their customs and traditions are still German. They brought cures and curses and recipes that were

Going Visiting by Richard Petri, c. 1855

older than the times of their grandparents. They brought their tools and ways of building houses and fences and furniture that would always tie their styles with the ways of the Old Country. They brought the bonding of their German lives that had been a part of their generations for centuries, and they mixed them with their new Texas environment and experiences. And out of this new German culture they created their own kind of Texas folklore.

"The German settlers had one thing in common, their sense of Germanness, their *Deutschtum,* an ethnic bond that both strengthened and isolated them. The German leaders during those early hard days of the 1840's and 1850's, when the settlers were just getting a toehold in the new land, believed that the physical survival of the German immigrants depended on their being bound together by their language, customs, and traditions, and cooperating as a result of this bonding and isolation. Prince Carl feared dilution of the German spirit and German ways more than he feared the hardships of the new land. He warned the settlers to stay away from Anglo-Americans and directed all settlements to begin with pure German stock. His despair was the loss of Germanic traditions of language and lifestyle in the New World, of Anglicizing names and of forgetting or renouncing the old customs." [65]

They neither renounced nor forgot. From the beginning they were different—more fun-loving and family-centered. Early Anglo-American settlers, those who held to their Puritan Sunday, were shocked by the way Germans observed the day. For the Germans Sunday was a day not only for worship but also for sports, competitions, clubs, and enjoyable family outings. A daughter-in-law of Adolphus Fuchs wrote, "We had fine times on Sundays and holidays when all assembled at the grandparents', for they always had plenty of fish and venison roast, and Grandmother always had something good in addition to that. The best was the coffee for afternoon lunch, and the music that followed it, and the stimulating conversation."

According to some Anglo-American observers, the Germans even drank and danced on Sundays. The Germans, however, would have it no other way, Sunday or any day of the week. "Now I began to feel rather proud of my success and my achievements," wrote Max Krueger, "and it was my intuition to attempt to transplant German cordiality and sociability in this foreign land. To this end I built a dance pavilion and bowling alley. The beer necessary for such occasions was imported from St. Louis." [66] Later Sundays became days of relaxation in parks and beer gardens.

The German immigrant showed his busy Anglo-American neighbor how to relax after toil, since what marked the German per-

San Antonio's Casino Bowling Team of 1899, an outgrowth of the athletic clubs, or Turnvereine, *brought to America by the immigrants of 1848*

haps most of all was his passion for "organized fun." Nothing was left to chance. An endless list of clubs, associations, societies, and fairs brought together men, women, children, and whole communities throughout the year. The Germans never did anything on a small scale, and, if interest lagged, competitions could be arranged between towns. Organizations kept German people together on a number of social levels. They were important traditions which the German Texan retained by making them into something Texan and American.

The German Union, founded in Houston in 1841, was the first of many fraternal, charitable, agricultural, athletic, political, theatrical, literary, singing, and dancing societies to be formed in Texas. Under a charter from the Texas Congress, the union assisted the sick and needy among German immigrants to the republic. Through such group activities, these people sought to perpetuate the social and cultural patterns of the fatherland, just as they attempted to preserve their language and literature by establishing their own schools, churches, and newspapers.

Masquerade balls, plays, concerts, song festivals, and competitions were held on special occasions and religious holidays. Many of these activities had their origin in European celebrations of the arrival of spring. The children's masquerade ball, or *Kindermaskenball*, of San Antonio was a part of the May festival. The children's masquerade ball of New Braunfels, on the other hand, was originally a part of

A Kindermaskenball of 1915

An early parade in New Braunfels

the pre-Lenten Fasching, or Mardi Gras, celebration. Both were accompanied by marches, dances, and parades in elaborate costumes.

Besides their own traditional *Maifest* and *Oktoberfest,* the German Texans celebrated the Fourth of July exuberantly. In New Braunfels an immigrant observed, "the Fourth of July celebration was held with games, music, and general merrymaking, in addition to a dance and the firing of a cannon in town. It was typical of the colonists that they should adopt the national holidays of the new country as their own." [67]

In another account from the Fredericksburg area, "We celebrated the Fourth of July in grand style. At seven in the morning, we all assembled on horseback at the club house. One man carried a flag which had been embroidered and decorated by the local ladies. We all rode leisurely towards Fredericksburg, and the procession grew steadily in size. Just before entering the town, we got into accurate formation and rode to the marketplace where members of the City Club were waiting for us. We were received with music and loud hurrahs! After about ten minutes, people came carrying a beautiful Texas flag. This had a large five-pointed star on top and the words 'Club of the Backwoodsmen.' The flagbearer was dressed in a blue denim shirt and trousers; he was an excellent representative for the backwoodsmen. We made a huge parade. A lot of people had assembled. Now some-

Cat Spring's huge octagonal pavilion built in 1902

Loesscher Band, Cat Spring

A German Day parade in La Grange

one read the 'Declaration of Independence' first in English and then in German. After that each family served refreshments to its members and their friends. Then we had target-shooting. Later the young people danced. At odd times there were shooting matches, foot races, and jumping matches. The winners had to pay for the wine, which all enjoyed very much. At four in the afternoon, there were speeches and after that they danced the polonaise. The gay life lasted until six the next morning—July 5th, when everybody had a cup of coffee." [68]

Recreation for the German Texans was not confined to major holidays. They turned all their clubs and even their work into organized entertainment. Groups like the Cat Spring Agricultural Society, founded in 1856, and the Germania Farmers' Verein of Anhalt, established in 1875, were intended to educate German farmers. An important secondary function, however, of these farming cooperatives was the planning of frequent dances and fairs. Eventually it was the dances, the social side of the meetings, that kept these organizations going as the agricultural functions became less important. Twice a year—Maifest and Harvest Festival—at Anhalt and monthly at Cat Spring, German brass "umpah-pah" bands and polka bands (now being supplanted gradually by popular country and western groups) still draw crowds numbering in the hundreds for dancing that lasts far into the night. These are essentially family affairs, with children, parents, grandparents, and great-grandparents sharing beer-drinking and fun-loving *Gemütlichkeit*. Behind all this was the extended family, a complex set of relationships which included three or more generations, aunts and uncles, cousins, nieces and nephews. The folklife of the German Texans centered on the family—its home, its work, and its "beloved language." These were the bases of customs; these preserved their traditions. The families were patriarchal, and older relatives occupied a position of honor in the family. Management of home and land passed gradually from the *Opa* to the *Papa* and from the *Oma* to the *Mama*. Still, the grandparents, the "old ones," were always consulted on important decisions. All family life was seen in a very personal way as the model of a larger pattern of life in which every part had its purpose and its time. From Germany the old ones brought along the notion that when an older relative died, a child was born to take his place. In rural communities where the population remained fairly constant from generation to generation, this sequence of life and death was often discussed. They respected it—it was a tradition.

Large families were another tradition. At the turn of the century, for example, 11 couples in one rural community had a total of

Large families—the Carl Goeth home near Marble Falls

90 children. Women in the extended families not only kept house and cooked for field crews but also took care of vegetable gardens, orchards, and the feeding of penned livestock—the last a practice which Anglo-Americans (whom these Germans derisively called "biscuits") considered especially repugnant. With the transition toward fewer children and the breakdown of the self-sufficient family, women also began to drive trucks and tractors in the fields and help with roundups. The men, however, never worked in the houses or yards, although the boys did help with such chores as chopping wood, killing chickens, and feeding the penned livestock. The men worked the fields, tended the pastured or range livestock, and did the fencing, building, and marketing.

In the early years, the families had formed their own militias. Later they independently organized harvesting and marketing cooperatives (wool and mohair pools, peach-growers' cooperatives, and businessmen's guilds) and other means of mutual support (like burial insurance and care for the aged).

Christmas and Easter were celebrated as church and family holidays, but the most important social events were birthdays, wed-

160

dings, and dances. "The center and symbol of the Family Cult is *Geburtstag* [birthday]," observed Vera Flach. "First you clean the house. Cleanliness here was not next to godliness. It *was* godliness. The windows were washed, drawers lined with fresh paper, closets straightened, silver polished, and floor waxed. After that the hostess cooked. Cookies were baked ahead, bread and cakes the day before, rolls and coffee on the natal day, when all the leaves were put in the table and the best linen laid out. Sometimes the birthday hostess spent a day in bed after her party. Relatives and close friends arrived about three o'clock; the children, after school was out. The guests sat in a large circle on the gallery (in summer). As each one came in, she made the rounds, shaking hands with one and all. (On leaving, this was repeated.) The conversation at my first few *Geburtstags* was quite difficult for me. They spoke in German and I understood most of it, but it was the things they talked about that threw me. They spoke of babies and food and the doings of their cousins and their uncles and their aunts.

"Most weddings were followed by a great brouhaha at one of the dance halls. A notice in the local paper announced the date of the ceremony and invited 'all friends and relatives' of the young couple to attend the reception at the dance hall. In the hall, often decorated with twisted streamers of crepe paper, there were huge stacks of man-sized sandwiches, cakes and cookies without number, pots of coffee and, of course, kegs of beer. An orchestra from some Hill Country town played old-time and new dance tunes. Gifts were not sent to the bride's home but were brought to the reception and piled on a couple of tables to be opened later when the band took a well-deserved intermission." [69]

Weddings were often followed by a shivaree, a modification of the *Polterabend*, which took place in Germany the night before the wedding, when the friends of the newlyweds celebrated an evening of fun at the young couple's expense.

The menfolk took part in shooting clubs, while the women belonged to German literary and service societies. Apart from cards and dominoes, the most prevalent pastimes at social gatherings were games of mimesis, pranks, and joking. These were especially popular among the men at harvest time, which—like butchering, canning, barn-raising, and quilting—took on secondary social functions.

For the men especially, the landscape was imbued with the qualities of the early settlers. Since these people were, in many cases, the first to acquire title to their previously unsettled land, they viewed it as an extension of the family and identified it with their names in everyday speech and in storytelling. Land division of family farms among heirs frequently caused serious strife.

Stories were linked to certain landmarks, giving a human identity or quality to the land: like the shortcut *Onkel* Henry took down the bald hillside in his wagon when he got angry while building a fence; the valley where someone was frightened by some wild animals; the buzzard roost where *Onkel* Louis sent city slickers one night to poach "turkeys" on his brother's land; the road where a rattlesnake struck the county commissioner's Model -T tire and blew up as the escaping air inflated the snake's body through its fangs; or the curve near the Rigi where an angry *Tante* Emilie caused the car to roll off the left embankment because she sat in the back seat behind her husband, thereby throwing the old car off-balance on the curve.

Farmsteads presented a picture of uniformity. Although house and barn were not under the same roof as they were in a German farm village, the house and surrounding outbuildings (barns with lofts, pigsties, smokehouse, chicken house, milking shed, blacksmith shop, outhouse, windmill and tankhouse, covered dipping vat, etc.) formed a tight cluster connected by pens, corrals, and fences leading out to fields and pastures.

The early houses were rough log cabins (which the Germans disliked), but these were replaced by substantial limestone, half-timber, or frame houses as soon as possible. Most of these rural houses used Anglo-American floor plans and building styles (five-room, L - or T-shape, with a large kitchen where most activities centered, and a cellar) and for the most part were not identified by German construction methods such as half-timbering. Many of the houses had half-stories where the children slept, sometimes accessible by outside stairs, and all of them had large front and back porches called "galleries." For the most part, rural homes seldom reflected any strong socio-economic differences among the people. In the cities, of course, that was not the case.

Other differences among the early families, however, led to two amusing social conventions. One of these was the notion of "family rank." Any marriage which united a man and woman of different social positions was viewed in two ways: for the spouse who was marrying "up," the marriage was advantageous, while, for the other spouse, it could involve a loss of face which had to be ignored. The second convention has been the frequent practice of explaining other people's bothersome behavior by claiming that their ancestors were crude, slow-witted, dishonest, or otherwise unpleasant. Since by now many of the families in each community are related through blood or marriage, this practice often involves using one's own ancestors or those of one's spouse in the ridicule.

Apart from stories that preserved the ancestral and traditional character of the community and imparted personal attributes to the land, another type of folk humor which contributed to the self-portrait of these people was a complex set of animal metaphors. Here in its simplest form one acquires an insight into the earthy humor of the German Texans. These terms, in particular, constitute shared understandings retained from the Old World, but, like the German language in general, they underwent modification in Texas.

Next to their own names and the names they have given to many places in Texas, their "beloved German" is the tradition that has preserved and unified the rich family folklife of these people. Like everything else that they retained, their German has taken on its own Texas character while leaving its mark at the same time on the English they speak.

Some of the better-educated Germans, who in Europe had spoken nothing but the most correct German, evidently took to the playful use of dialect in the New World. Just as Rosa von Roeder Kleberg observed about the clothing of her brothers, "they allowed their beards to grow and adopted the dress of Prussian peasants," [70] many of the more romantic Germans spoke what they called *Plattdeutsch* (Low German) or their local dialects in conversation with people of their own rank in Texas. More commonly, however, the diverse European backgrounds of the families necessitated the speaking of standard nondialectal German without many of the peculiarities of place or class that mark the German of more homogeneous enclaves in Texas. This language, cut off from its linguistic source two and three generations ago, has been modified, of course, by the English language, the new environment and technology, and the culture of the surrounding Anglo-American majority. In many respects, though, the modified standard German spoken today throughout Central and Southwest Texas is similar to rural European German.

"Surely," observed Joseph Wilson, regarding the language in the eastern Texas counties of the German belt, "many Americans are unaware that generations of Texans, though native born, lived out their entire lives as Germans—that is, they spoke German in their homes; they had their own German community with their own churches and schools; their newspapers were in German; they were baptized, married, and buried in German (and the official documents of these events were in German); and their graves have inscriptions in their beloved mother tongue." [71]

163

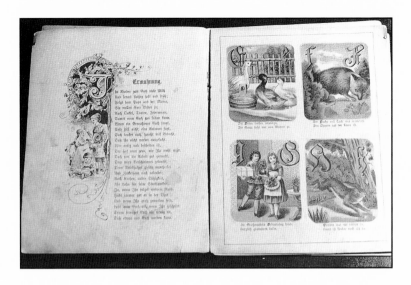

E, F, G, H *in a German primer at the Pioneer Memorial Museum, Fredericksburg*

In daily conversation, in popular song, in literature, and especially in sermons and hymns, the language bound them to their families, to their memories, and to their traditions. A father, writing in 1859, commented that his young son occasionally mixed Spanish, German, and English. Today many German Texans hardly notice when they change from German to English and back to German—for example, *der Phone, der Store, die Road, Butchermesser, die Mosquito*—but the pronunciation is all German. To hear a German Texan speak of his *"Pickup,"* an Anglo-American would be convinced by the pronunciation that this was an authentic German word, used every day on the streets of Wetzlar, Giessen, or Marburg. One writer admitted quite candidly, "Some people had a pronounced accent in their English. Others had practically none. Many Germans confused *v* with *w*. 'Wery—wacation—walentine—woice.' There were some mistakes in English grammar. But never in German! Their German was beautiful and correct."

To hear their language spoken is to know that, despite these borrowings, the German Texans resisted the melting pot, although, like all other ethnic groups, they contributed their own pieces to the mosaic of America—a nation of immigrants. The generations have maintained their *Deutschtum.* "There are no available statistics," wrote Vera Flach, wife of Professor Kapp's great-grandson, "but it is a shrewd guess that even today 70 percent of all German Americans still marry within the Germanic family, and this is the fifth (sometimes sixth) generation since pioneer days. The community approves of this. It keeps the bloodlines clean." [72] Behind it all is the language, the land, the ancestral home, the family, the dream, the magic West!

The insistence of these people upon improvement of the human condition made them "radicals" in a sense; then when they achieved here what they wanted, they became "conservative" in a desire to retain what they had found along with what they had preserved. We see the same people—radical in one situation, conservative in another. Often they had not changed a great deal—the set of values changed on them.

They were thoughtful people, and thoughtful people today do well to study them as an example from the past. Theirs is a history which personally explains the present. They tired of compromising with a deteriorating quality of life. Though they had no word in their native language for "frontier," they hoped to find amid the uncertainty of survival on the edge of the wilderness the certainty of their future. Like Americans in every century, this future lured them on and demanded great sacrifices of them. They began what other Americans began and have since continued—an endless immigration, or flight, into the future, always with the faith that today's problems may be solved tomorrow.

THE SONS OF HERMANN

The Order of the Sons of Hermann, the nation's oldest fraternal benefit society, was established in Texas by settlers in San Antonio on July 6, 1861. John Lemnitzer, who had been active in the Hermann Sons in New York, sought to form the San Antonio lodge in 1860, but authorization from the National Grand Lodge did not come until the next year. Hermann, for whom the Order was named, was an early German folk hero known as Hermann the Cherusker. He was captured by the Romans, then became a great leader of their army, and they Latinized his name to Arminius. However, when the Romans became particularly oppressive, Hermann forsook the glories of Rome, organized German tribesmen, and annihilated three Roman legions in the Battle of Teutoberg Forest in A.D. 9. He is honored still as one of the great German heroes of all time.

In 1890 a Grand Lodge of the Sons of Hermann was organized in San Antonio with eight member lodges across the state. It has grown, until now there are 160 lodges serving vast areas of Texas. In 1921 the Texas order became autonomous, and, by the early 1930's, it began conducting meetings in English.

The Sons of Hermann are engaged today in a wide variety of charitable or benevolent projects. One of their main functions has been to provide life insurance protection for members, a program started at a time when few people insured their lives. The lodges also stage or participate in *Volksfests,* concerts, dances, parades, and other public events.

In addition to providing insurance for members and their recreation and fellowship activities, the Sons of Hermann operate a youth summer camp and a home for the aged, both near Comfort, as well as schools of dance for junior members in many cities and towns.

RECREATION

*O*ne characteristic of European folklife in general was that these hardworking people made everyday tasks fun. "Every Thursday throughout the year, the men of the *Liedertafel* met at the Singers' Hall. Later there was a *Gemischte Chor,* a mixed chorus. The director was a man of modest means, a farmer with big, work-roughened hands. No matter how much there was to do on the farm, he came to town once a week with his violin, to teach four-part harmony to his singers. Farming was his livelihood, but music was his life. He and his wife went to operas and symphony concerts in the city fifty miles away with money that could have been spent for creature comforts. It never occurred to them to buy luxuries of any other kind.

"Sunday afternoon from March to October was the time set aside for the gun clubs. Like the *Liedertafel,* these clubs had been in existence from pioneer days. The target range was two hundred yards. Each club gave a monthly medal, but it had to be won three times in succession before a man could keep it.

"The men still shoot target on Sunday afternoons and polish off a keg of beer. There is still a *Sängerfest* every year, but not as large as it used to be. The *Geburtstag* is not quite so elaborate, but coffee and cake await the visitors who have remembered the day. And visiting will never change."

Vera Flach

167

German women gathered for coffee and conversation at their regular Kaffeklatsch, *or "coffee gossip," which turned into a kind of ladies' circle—for literature, fashions, recipes, or plain gossip. In addition to the standard fare of German coffee cakes, they sometimes ate creamy pastries, sweet rolls, cakes, cookies, and pies with their coffee.*

Picnics—for young people or harvesting or shearing crews—afforded simple pleasures without great expense.

Pinochle, skat, and dominoes ("42")

The domestic arts—embroidery, needlework, crocheting, tatting, knitting, weaving, and quilting—enhanced folklife and provided creative recreation.

"The mountain air was good for us all. We went on hunting parties for days at a time."

The Kammlah House in Fredericksburg (now the Pioneer Memorial Museum)

*First living quarters,
behind the old store*

THE GROWTH
OF A HOUSE

Second kitchen

*A*s they became prosperous, German settlers in the older areas along the Brazos began to have the ceilings and walls of their homes decorated with colorful designs. A number of artists did these striking decorations, some with stencils, some freehand. One of the finest was Rudolph Melchior, a successful artist who had emigrated from Germany. Melchior lived in Latium, a community of intellectuals in Washington County. The prime example of his artistry in decoration is preserved at the Lewis-Wagner farmstead in Winedale, restored by Miss Ima Hogg and given to The University of Texas. Other examples of his work are to be seen in Henkel Square restorations at Round Top.

FOUR PIONEERS DISCUSS MARRIAGE IN THE 1850's

All girls that fain would have a husband can confidently come to America. It borders on the ridiculous the way the Americans follow after the German girls.

Ida Kappel Kapp, 1850

In those days there was ample opportunity for a young lady to marry. There were hordes of cultured and attractive young men in Texas constantly on the lookout for wives. Young women, on the other hand, were scarce. There were only those who had immigrated to the state with their parents, none who had grown up in Texas.

Ottilie Fuchs Goeth, mid-1850's

Dear Father, you suggest that in choosing a wife I should keep an eye out for one with a good dowry. But in this country, I would be glad if I could find one that I could like and forget the dowry. Life with a housekeeper here would be distasteful to me, because I could not find a woman who would be suitable. Every nice girl gets married here at an early age, so that leaves only the undesirable ones and one of that kind could not be an efficient housekeeper. There are enough and pretty girls here, but the cultured and educated ones are rare, and it would be quite impossible for me to marry an uneducated person. Here in America a man's wife can influence . . . his career much more easily than in Germany, because here everybody depends entirely on himself. Even if there were a girl here with a dowry, she would be so conceited about it that it would only cause trouble.

Carl Hilmar Guenther, 1853

The early immigration consisted mainly of younger men of good families, many highly educated, who did not like the political and social conditions in Europe. Not until later did . . . farmers, artisans, and workers' families come, through the agency of the Adelsverein, people whom the country needed most of all. Because only few were cut out to be hermits, it often happened that men of scientific and social backgrounds married girls of the common people, whom they would not have introduced to their family circles across the ocean, but whose industry and practical sense were a good dowry in a country where little is to be had and the individual must provide for many things himself.

Emma Murck Altgelt, late 1850's

GERMAN FAMILY NAMES

German family names, like surnames from most European countries, fall generally into four categories. The oldest and one of the most common sources of German family names is the one which showed the origin of an individual. Families drew their surnames from any number of places: towns, buildings, streams, forests, and other geographic features.

A person acquired a surname from a town name in the following manner. There might have been three Johanns living in one place; everyone would have his own way of distinguishing between these three men in speech. If a fourth Johann would have moved to Berlin from Bremen, the fact that he had newly arrived in the town and *had come from a different place* could have been used to further identify the man, and the people of Berlin might have referred to him as "Johann from Bremen" (der Johann von Bremen), and eventually von Bremen or Bremer might have stuck for him and his family.

Several names of this type include Allerkamp, Bremer, Holekamp, Laubach, Neffendorf, Nürnberger, Weinheimer, and Wurzbach. All of these names came from German town and community names. However, people got their family names from other places as well. The names Bach (stream) and Wald (forest) are good examples showing where the individuals so described lived, as are Burg (castle), Kirchhoff (cemetery), Alberthal and Ranzau (with the references to the words *thal,* valley, and *au,* meadow), and Flach (plain).

Another way in which German names were acquired was through the occupation of the head of the family. If two men named Anton lived in a town, one could have been called Anton Weber (the weaver) and the other Anton Müller (the miller).

The list of occupational names is quite long. A Meyer was a master farmer; a Becker was a baker; a Bergmann was a coal miner; an Eisenhauer was an iron worker; a Metzger was a butcher; and a Zimmerman was a carpenter. Names like Ahlemeyer and Piepmeier are occupational names prefaced by the names of farms where these people lived.

Family names could also result from descriptions of someone's appearance or personality. Klein (short), Langbein (long leg), Rothwangl (red cheek), Schwarz (black), Fuchs (fox), Hahn (rooster), Nimitz (the Slavic name for German), and Ernst (serious) fall into this third category.

The last group of German names derived from the father's first name. Jakob Friedrichs was Jakob, son of Friedrich. Hansen came from Hans's or Johann's son; Heiner came from Heinrich's son, and Jacobi or Jakobson from Jakob's son. Others in this category are Dietz, Gunther, and Hermann.

Some names were much more acceptable than the majority of other names. Prestige was attached to surnames like Vogt (bailiff), Richter (judge), and Schulz (mayor).

The authoritative reference work on German family names is by Brechenmacher and can be found in some libraries. The University of Texas at Austin has a copy of the work. It lists most German surnames which have ever existed, etymologies, variants, and the earliest written records of the surnames.

FRANZ HADDENBROCK
The Texas *Onkel*

A popular storyteller with young and old alike, Franz Haddenbrock was one of the distinctive "village types" which included town gossips, matchmakers eccentrics, ne'er-do-wells, and wheeler-dealers, as well as storytellers.

Julius Dresel's reminiscences describe the Texas *Onkel* in detail. "Haddenbrock joined me on my way to Behr's farm. This man was very popular among the Germans and at home on many farms in West Texas. He was noticeable for his long, yellow beard; large, round eyes; and extraordinarily long hooked nose, as well as for his somewhat bent carriage and the close-cropped hair on his head. He was quite a character, who had dealt in wines and survived three wives. At present, his philosophical attitude towards life caused his breath to smell slightly of whiskey, and his principal concern was to 'make his life' (get his living) with as little work as possible, in which he was remarkably successful. Occasionally he would go hunting. He did not allow himself to deteriorate entirely, was a loyal friend, and possessed many good qualities, with a great deal of sound sense."

TALES THE GERMAN TEXANS TELL

The Hackman and the Stranger

A stranger came to Berlin and hired a hackman to show him the sights of the city. The hackman began to point out the city's various buildings.

"That building is over a hundred years old," he said.

"How long did it take to build it?" asked the stranger.

"Ten years," said the hack driver.

"In my country, they could build it in two!" retorted the stranger.

"There is a famous building," said the hackman.

"How long did it take to build it?"

"Twenty years."

"In my country, we could do it in four!"

As the two passed through the city, the conversation continued in this manner. Each time the stranger said that the building could be made faster in his own country. Then they came to the largest building in the city.

"How long did it take you to build that?" demanded the stranger.

The hack driver looked at it in disbelief and scratched his head.

"I don't know," he said, "but it wasn't here yesterday."

Collected by Carolyn Mankin

The Donkey Is a Dumb, Laughable Animal

The German spoken in Texas abounds in earthy, humorous expressions. Along with their fondness for storytelling and proverbs, the German speakers have retained at least a hundred expressions to describe people in animal terms. These animal metaphors belong to an old peasant vocabulary used to describe a wide variety of personalities and to put people in their place.

The assumption that a donkey is a dumb, laughable animal underlies the opinion one may have that his neighbor is as stupid and ridiculous as a donkey. Usually such opinions remain unexpressed, but, if one is pushed too far, one might retaliate by shouting, "Du Esel!"—"You donkey!" Although not a deadly insult, as some of the metaphors are, this one can serve the function of "correcting" another person's bothersome conduct. Of course, it is particularly funny to anyone else who witnesses the outburst.

Two popular examples of these animal metaphors are *Schweinehund* and *Schmeichelkätzchen*. When not used merely in joking, *Schweinehund* implies a mean and repulsive man, although literally it means "swine-dog." *Schmeichelkätzchen* means "sweet-talking kitten" and is used to describe a female who tells people just the things they want to hear, a flatterer or a coquette. Like stories and proverbs, these animal metaphors belong to the collected folk wisdom. The social values they enforce are the positive values of the German. Anyone who pushes other people too far or who causes tension in his family or community can become the target of these expressions.

Proverbs and Folk Wisdom

"Well begun is half done."

"If the roosters crow after dark, rain will come."

"Work makes life sweet."

"If snails crawl up the side of the house, rain is coming."

"What little Hans doesn't learn, big Hans will never learn."

"If you dream that you were bitten by a rattlesnake, you will
     have bad luck."

"Thistles bear no grapes."

"If you wink at a girl, she will become your sweetheart."

"Bright flowers have no scent."

"If rain falls during a funeral, one of those present
     will soon die."

"Time brings wisdom."

"A horseshoe hung in a fruit tree will make the tree bear and
     prevent its freezing."

"Everything depends on God's blessing."

"What good is a pretty bowl if it is empty."

From collections by E.R. Bogusch, Gilbert Jordan,
and Curt Schmidt

GERMAN FOLK IN TEXAS
An Essay in Pictures

*W*hen I close my eyes, I can see a sort of montage—families coming to the dance with babies and blankets for them to sleep on—big German feather beds—men's voices raised in song at a cafe, *'Er lebe hoch, er lebe hoch!'*—and food, food, food. There were great loaves of brown bread and homemade butter, venison and pork sausage, sweet-sour dishes, *Kochkäse,* cakes and cookies without number.

Vera Flach

Fredericksburg Tapestry
Pioneer Memorial Museum

*T*he cedar tree from the family ranch stood ablaze with candles in tin holders that had come from Germany with Oma's family. The tree bore cookies covered with glittering colored sugar and baked with hooks embedded in them, oranges, apples and porous net stockings holding gay, hard candies hung on many limbs. Each family had at least a few delicate decorations, treasured and hoarded carefully from year to year." [73]

"The word *Christmas* as used in our village was somewhat confusing. If I were asked to come over on Christmas, this did not mean December 25. Christmas Day meant the 25th. The 24th was a night of great activity. Supper was early. There was homemade wine, herring salad and black-eyed peas for good luck as well as the usual bountiful repast. If there were small children, the living room was kept tightly closed except when adults slipped through doors opened only a crack. In some families a bell was rung to show that Santa Claus was departing." [74]

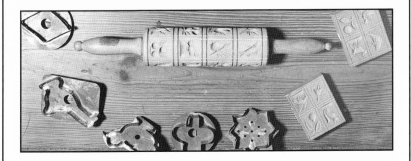

The Waltz

German women introduced this cultivated dance form to Texas towns and cities.

Cards, Dominoes, and Singing

"Singing was heard in the cafes where the men gathered to drink beer and play pinochle and skat. Here the singing went on late into the night, all the old nostalgic melodies of the Fatherland." [75]

"Authentic Texas barbecue grew up in German farming communities of Central Texas. Small-town meat markets satisfied the hunger of Saturday shoppers who converged from the surrounding countryside."

Atlantic Monthly, 1975

Some German Specialities

Kaffeekuchen
Streusselkuchen
Apfelstrudel
Streusselschnecken
Elefantenohren

Kartoffelpuffer (Potato Cakes)
6 medium potatoes
1 tsp. salt
2 eggs
½ c. flour
1 tsp. baking powder

     Peel and finely grate raw potatoes. Add salt and beaten eggs. Sift in flour and baking powder. Mix and shape into little cakes (like hot cakes) with a strip of bacon on top. Fry in hot shortening or butter, turning once. Serve hot. [76]

"Cabbage Loaf, Wine Soup, *Kochkäse, Pannas,* Coconut Pie, *Zwieback,* Christmas cookies *(Pfeffernüsse,* molasses and honey cookies, *Makronen),* turkey dressing made with raisins, and fairly sweet, German brown bread." [77]

Smokehouse on a German ranch

EASTER FIRES

An enduring Hill Country legend came about as a continuation of an old German tradition onto which the Meusebach-Comanche negotiations were grafted. While John O. Meusebach and his men were traveling into the Indian hunting lands, according to popular Hill Country stories, the Indians themselves placed guards around the town of Fredericksburg to ensure against the white man's treachery. They built signal fires on the hills overlooking the town. As long as the fires blazed high, the tribesmen in the distant camps knew that all was well.

The children in the German settlement were frightened when they saw the fires, but a pioneer mother fabricated a story that it was only the Easter rabbit at work, boiling eggs in great cauldrons and then dyeing them with wildflowers gathered from the hills. The custom of the annual fires, prevalent in many parts of Europe, has been continued at Fredericksburg in a colorful pageant enacted by descendants of the pioneers.

OLD AND NEW TRADITIONS
Fairs, May Dances, *Oktoberfests*

New Braunfels Conservation Society Gartenfest

Germania Farmers' Verein dance, Anhalt

armers' associations like the Germania Farmers' Verein at Anhalt provide relaxation and fun for rural people. The May and October Anhalt dances, a long-standing tradition of the Comal-Kendall County area, are this kind of carefree event, complete with music, food, and beer.

New Braunfels's German consciousness peaks for ten days at the end of October and the beginning of November for the rousing Wurstfest. This popular celebration, the most famous of the German-Texan festivities, draws thousands of singing, dancing, and drinking participants.

In Boerne, where the main street's Western stores sit side by side with stone houses and prim gardens reminiscent of the Old World, an annual Berges-Fest is held each June. Like the European town fairs after which it is patterned, this festival includes parades, games, music, and exhibits.

A GERMAN LEGACY IN TEXAS PLACE-NAMES

Archer County
   Windthorst
Austin County
   Millheim
Baylor County
   Fulda
Bexar County
   Elmendorf
Brazos County
   Kurten
Caldwell County
   Uhland
Colorado County
   Blumenthal
   Frelsburg
   Weimar
Comal County
   Anhalt
   Bracken
   Fischer Store
   Freiheit
   Gruene
   Kleinjohann
   New Braunfels
   Schoental
   Solms
   Startzville
   Ufnau
   Vogel Valley
   Walhalla (now Sattler)
   Wenzel
Cooke County
   Muenster
DeWitt County
   Arneckeville
   Hochheim
   Lindenau
   Meyersville
   Nordheim
Erath County
Falls County
   Westphalia
Fayette County
   Biegel
   Blum Hill

Ellinger
Engle
Flatonia
Freyburg
Nassau Farm
Oldenburg
Schulenburg
Swiss Alp
Waldeck
Walhalla
Warda
Gillespie County
   Albert
   Blumenthal
   Eckert
   Fredericksburg
   Klein-Frankreich
   Kreuzberg
   Luckenbach
   Mecklenburg
   Nebgen
   Rheingold
   Wrede
Goliad County
   Schroeder
Guadalupe County
   Barbarossa
   New Berlin
   Schertz
   Schumannsville
   Weinert
   Zorn
   Zuehl
Hays County
   Niederwald
Jones County
   Luedens
Karnes County
   Runge
Kendall County
   Bergheim
   Boerne
   Jungfrau
   Lindendale
   Rigi

Kerr County
  Dickeberg
  Hannischenkopf
  Hasenwinkel
  Spitzeberg
  Wolkenberg
  Zanzenberg (now Center Point)
Kleberg County
  Vatmannville
Knox County
  Rhineland
Lavaca County
  Breslau
  Henkhaus
  Vienna
  Wied
Lee County
  Fedor
  Germania
  Loebau
  Manheim
  Serbin
Llano County
  Bettina
  Castell
  Leiningen
  Meerholz
  Schoenburg
Martin County
  Marienfeld
Mason County
  Bodeville

Grossville
Hedwig's Hill
Hilda
Hoersterville
Plehweville
Simonville
Midland County
  Germania (now Paul)
Randall County
  Umbarger
Real County
Robertson County
  New Baden
Schleicher County
Stonewall County
  Brandenburg
    (now Old Glory)
Tom Green County
  Scherz
Travis County
  Dessau
  Pflugerville
Uvalde County
  Knippa
Washington County
  Berlin
  Latium
  Rehberg
Williamson County
  Schwertner
  Walburg

THE FAMILY

The Chris Lindemann Family in 1900

irst I learned that the German-American people whose fore-bears had been Texas pioneers had one great central creed. It was woven into the very fabric of their being. All other characteristics stemmed from it. It motivated everything they did. This central theme was *Family.*

Vera Flach

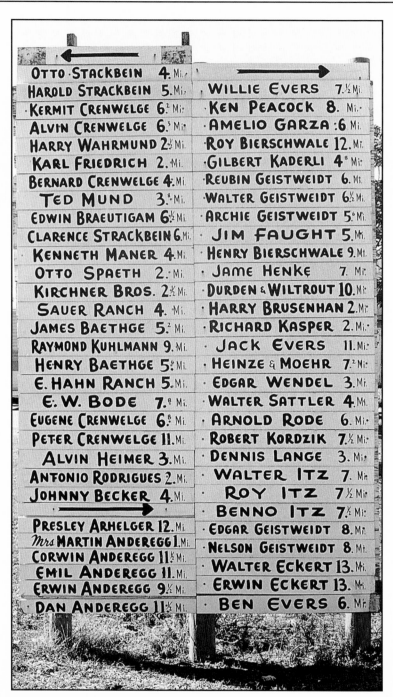

OTTO STACKBEIN 4. Mi.
HAROLD STRACKBEIN 5. Mi.
KERMIT CRENWELGE 6.² Mi.
ALVIN CRENWELGE 6.³ Mi.
HARRY WAHRMUND 2½ Mi.
KARL FRIEDRICH 2. Mi.
BERNARD CRENWELGE 4. Mi.
TED MUND 3.⁸ Mi.
EDWIN BRAEUTIGAM 6½ Mi.
CLARENCE STRACKBEIN 6. Mi.
KENNETH MANER 4. Mi.
OTTO SPAETH 2. Mi.
KIRCHNER BROS. 2½ Mi.
SAUER RANCH 4. Mi.
JAMES BAETHGE 5.² Mi.
RAYMOND KUHLMANN 9. Mi.
HENRY BAETHGE 5.⁸ Mi.
E. HAHN RANCH 5. Mi.
E. W. BODE 7.⁸ Mi.
EUGENE CRENWELGE 6.⁸ Mi.
PETER CRENWELGE 11. Mi.
ALVIN HEIMER 3. Mi.
ANTONIO RODRIGUES 2. Mi.
JOHNNY BECKER 4. Mi.

PRESLEY ARHELGER 12. Mi.
Mrs MARTIN ANDEREGG 1. Mi.
CORWIN ANDEREGG 11½ Mi.
EMIL ANDEREGG 11. Mi.
ERWIN ANDEREGG 9½ Mi.
DAN ANDEREGG 11½ Mi.

WILLIE EVERS 7½ Mi.
KEN PEACOCK 8. Mi.
AMELIO GARZA 6 Mi.
ROY BIERSCHWALE 12. Mi.
GILBERT KADERLI 4.⁸ Mi.
REUBIN GEISTWEIDT 6. Mi.
WALTER GEISTWEIDT 6½ Mi.
ARCHIE GEISTWEIDT 5.⁶ Mi.
JIM FAUGHT 5. Mi.
HENRY BIERSCHWALE 9. Mi.
JAME HENKE 7. Mi.
DURDEN & WILTROUT 10. Mi.
HARRY BRUSENHAN 2. Mi.
RICHARD KASPER 2. Mi.
JACK EVERS 11. Mi.
HEINZE & MOEHR 7.² Mi.
EDGAR WENDEL 3. Mi.
WALTER SATTLER 4. Mi.
ARNOLD RODE 6. Mi.
ROBERT KORDZIK 7½ Mi.
DENNIS LANGE 3. Mi.
WALTER ITZ 7. Mi.
ROY ITZ 7½ Mi.
BENNO ITZ 7½ Mi.
EDGAR GEISTWEIDT 8. Mi.
NELSON GEISTWEIDT 8. Mi.
WALTER ECKERT 13. Mi.
ERWIN ECKERT 13. Mi.
BEN EVERS 6. Mi.

Signpost, Doss

C H R O N O L O G Y
of Central European Colonization in Texas
Lera Patrick Tyler

	1831	Friedrich Ernst receives land at Mill Creek in Austin County and begins writing letters to friends in Oldenburg and Westphalia.
	1832	The German settlement of Biegel develops along Cummins Creek in Fayette County.
Renewal of Anglo-American colonization in Texas	1834	Several German families, including the Klebergs and the von Roeders, are encouraged by the Ernst letters to come to Texas. They settle at Cat Spring in Austin County.
Texas Independence	1836	
	1838	Friedrich Ernst founds the town of Industry in Austin County.
		William Frels establishes the German settlement of Frelsburg in the northern corner of Colorado County.
	1839	L.C. Ervendberg holds the first recorded religious services among the German Texans in Houston.
Texas government grants land contracts to immigrant agents.	1841	Charles Sealsfield (Karl Anton Postl) publishes *The Cabin Book*, a popular novel about Texas which had great influence on the immigration of German-speaking Europeans.
	1842	The *Adelsverein* (The Society for the Protection of German Immigrants in Texas) organizes at Biebrich on the Rhine near Mainz.
		Henri Castro contracts with the Texas government to establish a colony of 600 families.
	1842-45	Shelby (Roedersmühle) becomes a small German farm community in Austin County. A number of families sponsored by the Adelsverein populate the village in 1845 and 1846.

	1843	Count Boos Waldeck buys a plantation in Fayette County for the Adelsverein. On this purchase Nassau Farm, a "manor house" retreat for the society's officials, is built.
	1844	High Hill, first known as Oldenburg, Wursten, and Blum Hill, develops as a German community in southern Fayette County. In 1860, however, Czech families arrive there to start a Catholic settlement, the mother colony of Schulenburg.
Voyage from the Continent to Galveston or Indianola takes about 12 weeks.		Henri Castro lays out the town of Castroville west of San Antonio on the Medina River. By 1847 over 2,000 French, Alsatian, and German colonists live on Castro's grant.
	1845	Carl, Prince of Solms-Braunfels and first commissioner-general of the Adelsverein, founds the town of New Braunfels with about 200 German immigrants on Good Friday.
		Ross Prairie, another small German settlement, develops in eastern Fayette County.
		In Austin County, the German community of Millheim, an offshoot of Cat Spring, grows as some Adelsverein settlers venture into the more populous eastern regions of Texas.
		Johan Reinert Reiersen's colony of Normandy in Henderson County attracts Norwegian immigrants.
	1845-50	New Ulm is settled by former inhabitants of Nassau, Industry, and Shelby.
Annexation of Texas	1846	Baron Ottfried Hans von Meusebach, second commissioner-general for the Adelsverein, leads German families farther into the Hill Country of western Texas to establish Fredericksburg.
United States and Mexico at war		The *Galveston Zeitung,* the first German newspaper in Texas, begins publication.
	1846-47	Geologist Ferdinand Roemer visits the German-populated areas of Texas, recording his scientific and personal observations.

	1847	Meusebach ventures into Indian territory to conclude a treaty with the Comanches allowing Germans to settle on Indian lands.

"The Forty," a fraternity of young students under the leadership of Dr. Ferdinand von Herff and Gustav Schleicher, establish communistic Bettina on the north bank of the Llano River.

Four other settlements—Castell, Meerholz, Leiningen, and Schönburg— are attempted by the Adelsverein on the lands of the Fisher-Miller grant.

The United States and Mexico conclude the Treaty of Guadalupe Hidalgo, ending Mexican claims to Texas and a large portion of western North America

1848

The Forty-Eighters, refugees from the revolution of 1848, arrive in Texas. A number of prominent and well-educated Germans from this group of refugees settle at Sisterdale on the Guadalupe.

The town of Yorktown in DeWitt County is planned and settled by Germans.

Swen Swenson returns to Texas with about 25 Swedes. Between this date and 1861, over 200 Swedes come to the state under the leadership of Swenson and his uncle Swante Palm.

1849

Victor Witte and other German intellectuals establish Latium in Washington County.

Germans compose approximately 20 percent of the white population of Texas. The boundaries of Texas are fixed by the U.S. Congress in the Compromise of 1850.

1850
1852

Five members of "the Forty" organize a German communistic farm named Tusculum, which develops into the town of Boerne in the Hill Country.

Sixteen Czech families journey inland to start the New Bremen community in Austin County. Fayetteville, originally a German town, becomes a center of Czech settlement.

Four Oldenburger schoolmasters establish the town of Welcome in northern Austin County.

Steamships begin to replace clippers in trans-Atlantic passenger traffic.

German farmers disperse from the towns first established by the *Adelsverein*. Small farm communities like the Cypress Creek settlement begin as these immigrants are drawn by cluster migration and by availability of land into the fertile river valleys.

The *Neu-Braunfelser Zeitung* starts publication with Ferdinand Lindheimer as editor.

1853

The first German-Texan *Sängerfest* is held at New Braunfels.

Der freie Verein organizes at Sisterdale. With Dr. Ernst Kapp as president, the society takes a strongly worded stand against slavery.

Dr. Adolf Douai edits the *San Antonio Zeitung*. A year before, he was driven from New Braunfels for his radical views, and in San Antonio he rouses the violent opposition of Southerners with his abolitionist platform.

Texas legislature sets aside $2,000,000 for a state school system, but not until the late 1800's does the system become a reality. Throughout the decade Germans call for compulsory public education.

1854

Ernst Hermann Altgelt organizes the Cypress Creek settlement as the town of Comfort, a community of freethinkers and political extremists.

Influenced by the socialistic philosophy of Fourier, 350 Frenchmen led by Victor Consideránt and Francis Cantagel found the north Texas community of La Réunion.

Norwegian immigrants acquire land in southwestern Bosque County and begin settling in that area, with the establishment of Norse.

Hermann Seele and others organize the New Braunfels Dramatic Society.

Pastor Johann Kilian brings a group of over 500 Wends seeking religious freedom from the area of Dauban (Saxony) to Texas. These colonists establish Serbin in present Lee County.

Father Leopold Moczygemba, a Silesian priest in New Braunfels and Castroville, along with John Twohig, a San Antonio merchant, bring Polish settlers to the confluence of the Cibolo and San Antonio Rivers.

Panna Maria, the first homogeneous Polish community in the Western

Hemisphere, is founded by 100 families from Upper Silesia.

The Deutsch Texanischer Sängerbund organizes.

1855   Swiss immigrants, led by Carl Burkli, settle with the French at La Réunion. Shortly afterward, these 25 Swiss settlers disband to form their own neighborhood in Dallas, which continues to draw Swiss to Texas.

Under the leadership of Father Felix Zwiardowski, the Parish of St. Stanislaus is established by Poles in Bandera.

A German settlement develops at Round Top in Fayette County.

The Polish Parish of St. Hedwig is founded by John Demmer.

1856   Near Schulenburg, Czech immigrants settle Navidad and rename it Dubina.

German Agricultural Society of Austin County is chartered at Cat Spring.

1857   The poet Johannes Romberg organizes the Prairieblume, a literary society for young German Texans near Black Jack Springs, Fayette County.

The German Casino Club of San Antonio forms to promote social entertainments.

1858   Praha (Prague), originally Mulberry, an Anglo-American settlement in southern Fayette County, develops as Czech immigration to the area continues to increase.

1859   The first Jewish congregation, with a membership derived from France, Alsace, Bavaria, and other German-speaking lands, is chartered in Houston.

Secession and Civil War   1861

Homestead Act   1862   In Comfort several hundred male Unionists reorganize the "Union Loyal League" into a German battalion with companies from Kendall, Gillespie, and Kerr Counties. When these counties are declared in open rebellion, the German cadre assembles for

		movement into Mexico and is ambushed by a massive Confederate force. This Battle of the Nueces eliminates what remains of the radical German element in Texas.
Reconstruction	1866	After 25 years of caring for Jewish and non-Jewish families in Galveston, the Hebrew Benevolent Society formally incorporates.
	1867	Mayor Wilhelm C.A. Thielepape founds San Antonio's Beethoven Männerchor.
First railroad connections between Texas and other states.	1872	Ernst Hermann Altgelt constructs a home on King William Street, starting a fashionable residential district for San Antonio's German elite.
	1873	Cestochowa, a filial of Panna Maria, is established by 40 Polish families.
Cattle drives become more profitable, and by 1885 millions of head of cattle are sent north.		
End of Reconstruction	1874	
Indian raids into Texas cease.	1875	
The sale of railroad lands stimulates settlement of western Texas. Approximately 32 million acres (an area the size of Alabama) were disposed of in this way.	1878	Swedes start coming to Texas again. By 1895 over 5,000 settlers join their predecessors in Houston, Austin, Manor, and Palm Valley.
	1880	Ten Swiss families settle on the Guadalupe River near Seguin. As with the other Swiss colonies in Texas, they quickly disperse to already established towns and cities.
Windmills appear in western Texas.	1880's	German farmers begin to settle the divides and plains of West Texas, where water is now available, turning their farm operations into ranches.
		Germans from Colorado County found Westphalia in Falls County.
	1881	The Texanischer Gebirgs-Sängerbund organizes.
	1889	Muenster and nearby Lindsay in Cooke County, founded by Emil and Carl Flusche, become the fourth and fifth

		German Catholic colonies started in the New World by six brothers from Westphalia.
	1890	The Grand Order of the Sons of Hermann, a benevolent fraternal society, organizes in San Antonio.
	1890'S	German farmers from the older colonies of eastern Texas move into the area around Rosenberg in Fort Bend County.
		A small group of Russian Germans leaves Rorbach, near the Black Sea in Russia, and settles at Hurnville, Clay County, Texas.
	1891	Father Joseph Reisdorff brings German Catholics from the Midwest to Windthorst in Archer County. By 1911 five other colonies are established by Father Reisdorff.
	1892	Kosciusko in Wilson County is founded by 65 Polish families.
	1903	German Lutherans settle southwestern Haskell and eastern Stonewall Counties where the towns of Brandenburg (renamed Old Glory during World War I) and Sagerton develop.
	1905	German-speaking Mennonite congregation (16th century Swiss Anabaptist origin) is established at Tuleta, Bee County, Texas.
	1910	Germans primarily from out-of-state are attracted to the southern regions of Texas. Forty German Catholic families from the North settle Vatmannville in Kleberg County.
	1911	Deutschburg near Matagorda Bay is founded by Pastor Gerhard, a Lutheran minister from Wisconsin, and settled by Germans from the Midwest. Pastor Gerhard was only partially successful in his plan to create a health resort and gardening center there.
	1911-14	A larger body of German Mennonites settles temporarily in Dimmit County.
World War I	1915-18	One hundred sixty German Mennonites establish a colony near Littlefield.

Abernethy, Francis E. *"Deutschtum* in Texas: A Look at Texas-German Folklore." *German Culture in Texas: A Free Earth; Essays from the 1978 Southwest Symposium.* Ed. Glen E. Lich and Dona B. Reeves. Boston: Twayne, 1980, pp. 203-26.

_____. "Texas Folklore and German Culture." *Texas and Germany: Crosscurrents.* Ed. Joseph Wilson. *Rice University Studies* 63, no. 3 (1977): 83-99.

Alexander, Drury Blake. *Texas Homes of the Nineteenth Century.* Austin: University of Texas Press, 1966.

Alexander, Frances. *Orphans on the Guadalupe.* Quanah-Wichita Falls: Nortex, 1971.

Altgelt, Emma Murck. "Sketches of Life in Texas." Tr. and ed. H. Dielmann. *American-German Review* 26 (1960): 40.

√ Arndt, Karl John Richard. *German-American Newspapers and Periodicals. 1732-1955: History and Bibliography.* 2nd ed. rev. New York: Johnson Reprint, 1965.

Ashford, Gerald. "Paintings of Old San Antonio." *San Antonio Express Magazine,* August 5, 1951.

Baron, Stanley. *Brewed in America: A History of Beer and Ale in the U.S.* Boston: Little, Brown, 1962.

Barry, Colman. *The Catholic Church and German Americans.* Milwaukee: Bruce, 1953.

Bartscht, Waltraud. " 'Da Waren Deutsche Auch Dabei!' The Story of a Texas-German Family." *Texas and Germany: Crosscurrents.* Ed. Joseph Wilson. *Rice University Studies* 63, no. 3 (1977): 35-46.

Beach, Walter, tr. and comp. *Souvenir of Golden Jubilee, Church of the Visitation, Westphalia, Texas, July 4 and 5, 1933.* From a German Diary by Martin Roessler. Austin: Capital, 1933.

Benjamin, Gilbert Giddings. *The Germans in Texas: A Study in Immigration.* Americana Germanica 11. Philadelphia: University of Pennsylvania; New York: D. Appleton, 1909; rpt. Austin: Jenkins, 1974.

Bennet, Marion T. *American Immigration Policies: A History.* Washington, D.C.: Public Affairs Press, 1964.

Bennett, Bob. *Kerr County, Texas. 1856-1956.* San Antonio: Naylor, 1956.

Bestor, Arthur. *Backwoods Utopias: The Sectarian and Owenite Phases of Communitarian Socialism in America. 1663-1829.* Philadelphia: University of Pennsylvania Press, 1950.

Bewie, William Henry. *Missouri in Texas: A History of the Lutheran Church—Missouri Synod in Texas. 1855-1941.* Austin: n.p., 1952.

Bierschwale, Margaret. "Mason County, Texas. 1845-1860." *Southwestern Historical Quarterly* 52 (1940): 379-97.

Biesele, Rudolph L. "Dr. Ferdinand Roemer's Account of the Llano-San Saba Country." *Southwestern Historical Quarterly* 62 (1958): 71-74.

_____. "The First German Settlement in Texas." *Southwestern Historical Quarterly* 34 (1931): 334-39.

_____. "The German Settlers and the Indians in Texas, 1844-1860." *Southwestern Historical Quarterly* 31 (1927): 116-29.

_____. *The History of the German Settlements in Texas, 1831-1861.* Austin: Von Boeckmann-Jones, 1930.

_____. "Prince Solms' Trip to Texas. 1844-1845." *Southwestern Historical Quarterly* 40 (1936): 1-25.

_____. "The Texas State Convention of Germans in 1854." *Southwestern Historical Quarterly* 33 (1930): 247-61.

Biggers, Don H. *German Pioneers in Texas.* Fredericksburg: Fredericksburg Publishing Co., 1925.

Billigmeier, Robert Henry. *Americans from Germany: A Study in Cultural Diversity.* Belmont: Wadsworth, 1974.

Blumberg, Carl. "The True Effectiveness of the Mainz Society for Emigration to Texas as Described in a Letter of November 3, 1846." *Texana* 7 (1969): 295-312.

Blume, Irwin H. *The First Hundred Years of the "Schuhmann" Family of Fayette County, Texas.* Bellaire: Blume, 1973.

Bogusch, E.R. "Superstitions of Bexar County." Publications of the Texas Folklore Society 5 (1926): 112-25.

Bohmfalk, John Henry. *The History of the Friede Bohmfalk Family, Nov. 7, 1848 to Aug. 21, 1966.* San Antonio: n.p., 1966.

Bollaert, William. *William Bollaert's Texas.* Ed. W. Eugene Hollon and Ruth Lapham Butler. The American Exploration and Travel Series 21. Norman: University of Oklahoma Press, 1956.

Boot, Christine. "Home and Farm Remedies and Charms in a German Manuscript from a Texas Ranch." *Paisanos.* Publications of the Texas Folklore Society 41. Austin: Encino, 1978, pp. 111-31.

Bracht, Viktor. *Texas in 1848.* Tr. and ed. Charles Frank Schmidt. San Antonio: Naylor, 1931.

Branda, Eldon S. , ed. *The Handbook of Texas.* Vol 3. Austin: Texas State Historical Association, 1976.

Brechenmacher, Josef Karlmann. *Etymologisches Wörterbuch der deutschen Familiennamen.* Limburg an der Lahn: Starke, 1960-1963.

Brown, John Henry. *Indian Wars and Pioneers of Texas.* Austin: L.E. Daniell, 1890.

Carl, Prinz zu Solms-Braunfels. *Texas. 1844-1845.* Houston: n.p., 1936.

Carroll, H. Bailey. *Texas County Histories: A Bibliography.* Austin: Texas State Historical Association, 1943.

Cassdorph, Paul. *History of the Republican Party in Texas. 1865-1965.* Austin: Pemberton, 1965.

Cat Spring Agricultural Society. *The Cat Spring Story.* San Antonio: Lone Star, 1956.

____. *Century of Agricultural Progress. 1856-1957.* Tr. A.L. Schuette, E.P. Krueger, and E.A. Miller. San Antonio: Lone Star, 1956.

Chabot, Frederick C. *With the Makers of San Antonio: genealogies of the early Latin, Anglo-American, and German families with occasional biographies, each group being prefaced with a brief historical sketch and illustrations.* Yanaguana Society publication 4. San Antonio: Artes Graficas, 1937.

Chambers, William Trout. *Texas—Its Land and People.* Austin: Steck, 1952.

Clark, Sara. "The Decoration of Graves in Central Texas with Seashells." *Diamond Bessie and the Shepherds.* Ed. Wilson M. Hudson. Publications of the Texas Folklore Society 36 (1972): 33-43.

Comfort Middle School. *Those Comforting Hills.* 2 annotated vols. Comfort: Comfort News, 1975.

Coppa, Frank J., and Thomas Curran, eds. *The Immigrant Experience in America.* The Immigrant Heritage of America. Boston: Twayne, 1976.

Day, James M. *The Map Collection of the Texas State Archives. Maps of Texas. 1827-1900.* Austin, 1964.

Dielmann, Henry B. "Dr. Ferdinand Herff, Pioneer Physician and Surgeon." *Southwestern Historical Quarterly* 57 (1954): 265-84.

____. "Elizabeth Ney, Sculptor." *Southwestern Historical Quarterly* 45 (1961): 157-83.

____. "Emma Altgelt's Sketches of Life in Texas." *Southwestern Historical Quarterly* 63 (1959-1960): 363-84.

Dietrich, Wilfred O. *The Blazing Story of Washington County.* Brenham: Banner-Press, 1950; rev. ed., Wichita Falls: Nortex, 1973.

Douglass, Paul F. *The Story of German Methodism: Biography of an Immigrant Soul.* New York: Methodist Book Concern, 1939.

Dresel, Gustav. *Gustav Dresel's Houston Journal: Adventures in North America and Texas. 1837-1841.* Tr. and ed. Max Freund. Austin: University of Texas Press, 1954.

Ehrenberg, Hermann. *With Milam and Fannin: Adventures of a German Boy in Texas' Revolution.* Tr. Charlotte Churchill; ed. Henry Smith. Austin: Pemberton, 1968.

El-Beheri, Mary Mathis, et al. "We Love You, Julius!" *Retrospect and Retrieval: The German Element in Review. Essays on Cultural Preservation.* Ed. Dona B. Reeves and Glen E. Lich. Ann Arbor: University Microfilms International, 1978, pp. 83-139.

Elliott, Claude. "Union Sentiment in Texas. 1861-1865." *Southwestern Historical Quarterly* 50 (1946-1947): 449-77.

Erath, George Bernard. *Memoirs of Major George Bernard Erath.* Dictated to and arranged by Lucy A. Erath. Austin: Texas State Historical Association, 1923.

Erickson, Charlotte. *American Industry and the European Immigrant. 1860-1885.* Cambridge: Harvard University Press, 1957.

Estill, Julia. "Children's Games." *The Sky Is My Tipi.* Ed. Mody C. Boatright. Publications of the Texas Folklore Society 22. Austin: Texas Folklore Society, 1949, pp. 231-36.

_____. "Customs among the German Descendants of Gillespie County (in 1923)." *The Folklore of Texan Cultures.* Ed. Francis E. Abernethy. Publications of the Texas Folklore Society 38. Austin: Encino, 1974. The same essay appears in *Coffee in the Gourd.* Publications of the Texas Folklore Society 2 (1923); facsimile rpt. Dallas: Southern Methodist University Press, 1969.

_____. "The Enchanted Rock in Llano County." *Legends of Texas.* Ed. J. Frank Dobie. Publications of the Texas Folklore Society 3. Austin: Texas Folklore Society, 1924, pp. 153-56.

_____. *Fredericksburg, in the Texas Hill Country.* Comp. and issued by Fredericksburg Chamber of Commerce. Fredericksburg: Fredericksburg Publishing Co., 1946.

Etzler, T. Herbert. "German-American Newspapers in Texas with Special Reference to the *Texas Volksblatt. 1877-1879.*" *Southwestern Historical Quarterly* 57 (1954): 423-31.

Faust, Albert Bernhardt. *The German Element in the United States with Special Reference to Its Political, Moral, Social, and Educational Influence.* 2 vols. Boston: Houghton Mifflin, 1909.

Flach, Vera. *A Yankee in German America: Texas Hill Country.* San Antonio: Naylor, 1973.

Foik, Paul Joseph. *Early Plans for the German Catholic Colonization of Texas.* Austin: Texas Catholic Historical Society, 1934.

Fornell, Earl. "The German Pioneers of Galveston Island." *American German Review* 22 (1956): 15-17.

Franke, Gertrude. *A Goodly Heritage: The Story of Carl Siegesmund Bauer and His Descendants (1792-1975).* San Antonio: Alamo Printing, 1975.

Frantz, Joe B. "Ethnicity and Politics in Texas." *German Culture in Texas. A Free Earth, Essays from the 1978 Southwest Symposium.* Ed. Glen E. Lich and Dona B. Reeves. Boston: Twayne, 1980, pp. 191-202.

Friesen, Gerhard. "Adolph Douai's Literary Activities." *Journal of German-American Studies* 13 (1978): 25-38.

_____, and Walter Schatzberg, eds. *The German Contribution to the Building of the Americas.* Studies in Honor of Karl J.R. Arndt. Hanover: Clark University Press, 1977.

Fuchs, John R. *A Husband's Tribute to His Wife.* San Antonio: Naylor, 1938.

Fuchs, Louise Romberg. *Reminiscences (Erinnerungen).* Tr. Gertrude Franke. San Antonio: n.p., 1936.

Fuhrmann, Joseph P. *A Golden Jubilee History of the Sacred Heart Parish. 1889-1939. Muenster, Texas.* San Antonio: Standard, 1939.

Gallegly, Joseph S. "The Renaissance of the Galveston Theatre: Henry Greenwall's First Season. 1867-1868." *Southwestern Historical Quarterly* 62 (1958): 442-56.

Geiser, Samuel Wood. "Dr. Ernst Kapp, Early Geographer in Texas." *Field and Laboratory* 14, no. 1 (1946): 16-31.

_____. *Naturalists of the Frontier.* 2nd ed. rev. and enl. Dallas: Southern Methodist University Press, 1948.

Geue, Chester William, and Ethel Hander Geue. *A New Land Beckoned. German Immigration to Texas, 1844-1847.* Enl. ed. Waco: Texian, 1972.

Geue, Ethel Hander. *New Homes in a New Land. German Immigration to Texas: 1847-1861.* Waco: Texian, 1970.

Gilbert, Glenn, ed. *The German Language in America: A Symposium.* Austin: University of Texas Press, 1971.

_____. "The German Language in Texas: Some Needed Research." *German Culture in Texas: A Free Earth; Essays from the 1978 Southwest Symposium.* Ed. Glen E. Lich and Dona B. Reeves. Boston: Twayne, 1980, pp. 229-40.

———. *Linguistic Atlas of Texas.* Austin: University of Texas Press, 1972. (Deutscher Sprachatlas: Regionale Sprachatlanten, no. 5).

———. "Origin and Present-Day Location of German Speakers in Texas: A Statistical Interpretation." *Texas and Germany: Crosscurrents.* Ed. Joseph Wilson. *Rice University Studies* 63, no. 3 (1977): 21-34.

———. *Texas Studies in Bilingualism: Spanish, French, German, Czech, Polish, Serbian and Norwegian in the Southwest.* Studia Linguistica Germanica 3. Berlin: De Gruyter, 1970.

Gillespie County Historical Society. *Pioneers in God's Hills: A History of Fredericksburg and Gillespie County. People and Events.* 2 vols. Austin: Von Boeckmann-Jones, 1960, 1974.

Goeth, Ottilie Fuchs. *Memoirs of a Texas Pioneer Grandmother (Was Grossmutter Erzählt); 1805-1915.* Tr. Irma Goeth Guenther. Austin: n.p., 1969; rpt. Burnet: Eakin, 1982.

Goetzmann, William. *The American Hegelians: An American Intellectual Episode in the History of Western America.* New York: Knopf, 1973.

———. *Exploration and Empire: The Explorer and the Scientist in the Winning of the American West.* New York: Knopf, 1966.

Greeley, Andrew M. *Ethnicity in the United States: A Preliminary Reconnaissance.* New York: Wiley, 1974.

Greene, A.C. *The Last Captive: The Lives of Herman Lehmann.* Austin: Encino, 1972.

Greer, Georgeanna H., and Harding Black. *The Meyer Family: Master Potters of Texas.* San Antonio: Trinity University Press, 1971.

Groos, Anna Willrich. *Recollections.* Tr. Minnie Groos Wilkins. San Antonio: n.p., 1953.

Guenther, Carl Hilmar. *Diary and Letters.* Tr. Regina Beckmann Hurst. San Antonio: Clegg, 1952.

Haas, Oscar. *A Chronological History of the Singers of German Songs in Texas.* New Braunfels: Zeitung, 1948.

———. *The First Protestant Church: Its History and Its People. 1845-1955.* New Braunfels: Zeitung, 1955. *Supplement. 1955-1965.* New Braunfels: n.p., 1965.

———. *The History of New Braunfels and Comal County, 1844-1946.* Austin: Steck, 1968.

Hagen, Victor von. *The Germanic People in America.* Norman: University of Oklahoma Press, 1976.

Hale, Leon. "A Lesson on Playing Mühle." *Some Still Do.* Publications of the Texas Folklore Society 39. Austin: Encino, 1975, pp. 74-76.

Handlin, Oscar. *The Uprooted: The Epic Story of the Great Migrations that Made the American People.* Boston: Little, Brown, 1951.

Hasskarl, Robert A. *Brenham, Texas, 1844-1958.* Brenham: Banner-Press, 1958.

Heinen, Hubert. "Autobiography. Comfort, Texas. 1872-1965." Copy in the Learning Resources Center, Southwest Texas State University, San Marcos.

Heinen, Hubert P. "The Function of the German Literary Heritage." *German Culture in Texas: A Free Earth; Essays from the 1978 Southwest Symposium.* Ed. Glen E. Lich and Dona B. Reeves. Boston: Twayne, 1980, pp. 157-75.

Hendricks, Gordon. *Albert Bierstadt, Painter of the American West.* New York: Harry N. Abrams and Amon Carter Museum of Western Art, 1974.

Herff, Ferdinand Charles von. *The Regulated Emigration of the German Proletariat with Special Reference to Texas.* Tr. Arthur L. Finck. San Antonio: Trinity University Press, 1978.

Herff, Ferdinand Peter. *The Doctors Herff: A Three-Generation Memoir.* 2 vols. San Antonio: Trinity University Press, 1973.

Herminghouse, Patricia. "German-American Studies in a New Vein: Resources and Possibilities." *Die Unterrichtspraxis* 9 (1976): 3-14.

Herrmann, Maria. "The Restoration of Historical Fredericksburg." *Texas and Germany: Crosscurrents.* Ed. Joseph Wilson. *Rice University Studies* 63, no. 3 (1977): 119-39.

Hilda, Texas, Methodist Church. *History of the Hilda (Bethal) Methodist Church: Centennial. 1862-1962.* San Marcos: Record, 1962.

Hinüber, Caroline von. "Life of German Pioneers in Texas." *Quarterly of the Texas State Historical Association* 2 (1899): 227-32.

Hirschler, Eric. *Jews from Germany in the United States.* New York: Farrar, Straus and Cudahy, 1956.

History of the Pfluger Family. 1803-1978. Pflugerville: n.p., 1978.

Huber, Alvin O. "Frederick Armand Strubberg, Alias Dr. Shubbert: Townbuilder, Physician, and Adventurer. 1806-1866." *West Texas Historical Association Yearbook* 38 (1962): 37-41.

Huebener, Theodore. *The Germans in America.* Philadelphia: Chilton, 1962.

Hutson, Alice. *From Chalk to Bronze: A Biography of Waldine Tauch.* Austin: Shoal Creek, 1978.

Jackson, W.H., and S.A. Long. *The Texas Stock Directory or Book of Marks and Brands.* Vol. I. San Antonio: Herald, 1865.

Jenkins, John H. *Cracker Barrel Chronicle: A Bibliography of Texas Town and County Histories.* Austin: Pemberton, 1965.

Jordan, E.L. *America, Glorious and Chaotic Land: Charles Sealsfield Discovers the Young United States.* Englewood Cliffs: Prentice-Hall, 1969.

Jordan, Gilbert J. "German Cultural Heritage in the Hill Country of Texas." *German Culture in Texas: A Free Earth; Essays from the 1978 Southwest Symposium.* Ed. Glen E. Lich and Dona B. Reeves. Boston: Twayne, 1980, pp. 176-88.

_____. *German Texana: A Bilingual Collection of Traditional Materials.* Burnet: Eakin, 1980.

_____. "The Texas German Language of the Western Hill Country." *Texas and Germany: Crosscurrents.* Ed. Joseph Wilson. *Rice University Studies* 63, no. 3 (1977): 59-71.

_____. "Texas German Methodism in a Rural Setting." *Perkins Journal* 31, no. 3 (1978): 1-21.

_____. *Yesterday in the Texas Hill Country.* College Station: Texas A&M University Press, 1979.

_____, and Terry G. Jordan. *Ernst and Lisette Jordan: German Pioneers in Texas.* Austin: Von Boeckmann-Jones, 1971.

Jordan, Terry G. "Forest Folk, Prairie Folk: Rural Religious Cultures in North Texas." *Southwestern Historical Quarterly* 53 (1976): 135-62.

✓ _____. "The German Element in Texas: An Overview." *Texas and Germany: Crosscurrents.* Ed. Joseph Wilson. *Rice University Studies* 63, no. 3 (1977): 1-11. This is the definitive article-length treatment of German movement to and in Texas, along with discussions of cluster migration, dominant personalities, and immigrant letters.

_____. "German Folk Houses in the Texas Hill Country." *German Culture in Texas: A Free Earth; Essays from the 1978 Southwest Symposium.* Ed. Glen E. Lich and Dona B. Reeves. Boston: Twayne, 1980, pp. 103-20.

_____. "German Houses in Texas. . . ." *Landscape* 14 (1964): 24-26.

_____. *German Seed in Texas Soil: Immigrant Farmers in Nineteenth-Century Texas.* Austin: University of Texas Press, 1966.

✓ _____. "The German Settlement of Texas after 1865." *Southwestern Historical Quarterly* 73 (1969): 193-212.

_____. "The Old World Antecedent of the Fredericksburg Easter Fires." *The Folklore of Texan Cultures.* Ed. Francis E. Abernethy. Publications of the Texas Folklore Society 38. Austin: Encino, 1974, pp. 151-54.

_____. "The Pattern of Origins of the Adelsverein German Colonists." *Texana* 6 (1968): 245-57.

_____. "Perceptual Regions in Texas." *The Geographical Review* 68 (1978): 293-307.

_____. "Russian-German Folk House in North Texas." *Built in Texas.* Ed. Francis E. Abernethy. Publications of the Texas Folklore Society 42. Waco: E-Heart, 1979, pp. 136-38.

_____. *Texas Log Buildings: A Folk Architecture.* Austin: University of Texas Press, 1978.

Justman, Dorothy E. *German Colonists and Their Descendants in Houston, Including Usener and Allied Families.* Quanah: Nortex, 1974.

Keeth, Kent. "Sankt Antonius: Germans in the Alamo City in the 1850's." *Southwestern Historical Quarterly* 76 (1972): 183-202.

King, Irene Marschall. *Comanches on the Peace-Path.* Waco: Texian, 1970. This work is interesting because it shows a curiously ambivalent German attitude toward relations with the Indians which surfaces repeatedly in Texas-German lore.

_____. *John O. Meusebach: German Colonizer in Texas.* Austin: University of Texas Press, 1967.

Kleberg, Rosa von Roeder. "Some of My Early Experiences in Texas." *Quarterly of the Texas State Historical Association* 1 (1898): 297-302; 2 (1898): 170-73.

Kleberg, Rudolph. *Description of the Resources of DeWitt County, Texas. The Immigrant's Handbook. New Homes for the Industrious Farmers and Stockraisers.* Cuero: Cuero Star Office, 1887.

Kloss, Heinz. *Atlas of the 19th and 20th Century German-American Settlements.* Marburg: Elwert, 1974.

Koeltzow, Otto. "From the Brazos to the North Fork: The Autobiography of Otto Koeltzow. *Chronicles of Oklahoma* 40 (1962): 100-49.

Kowert, Art. "LBJ's Boyhood: Among the German-Americans in Texas." *American-German Review* 34 (1968): 2-6.

Kowert, Elise. *Old Homes and Buildings of Fredericksburg.* Fredericksburg: Fredericksburg Publishing Co., 1977.

Krueger, Max Amadeus Paulus. *Second Fatherland: The Life and Fortunes of a German Immigrant.* Ed. Marilyn McAdams Sibley. College Station: Texas A&M University Press, 1976. Originally published as *Pioneer Life in Texas: An Autobiography.* San Antonio: Clegg, 1930.

Lee County Historical Survey Committee. *History of Lee County, Texas.* Quanah: Nortex, 1974.

Lehmann, Winfred. "Lone Star German." *Texas and Germany: Cross-currents.* Ed. Joseph Wilson. *Rice University Studies* 63, no. 3 (1977): 73-81.

Lich, Glen E. "Balthasar Lich, German Rancher in the Texas Hills." *Texana* 12 (1974): 101-23.

———, and Dona B. Reeves, eds. *German Culture in Texas: A Free Earth; Essays from the 1978 Southwest Symposium.* Boston: Twayne, 1980. Lich contributed an essay to this collection entitled "Goethe on the Guadalupe," pp. 29-71.

———, and Lera Tyler Lich. "When the Creeks Run Dry: Water Milling in the German Hill Country." *Built in Texas.* Ed. Francis E. Abernethy. Publications of the Texas Folklore Society 42. Waco: E-Heart, 1979, pp. 236-45.

Lomax, Alan, and Sidney Robertson. *American Folksong and Folklore: A Regional Bibliography.* New York: Progressive Education Association, 1942.

Lotto, Frank. *Fayette County: Her History and Her People.* Schulenburg: the Author, 1902.

Malsch, Brownson. *Indianola: The Mother of Western Texas.* Austin: Shoal Creek, 1977.

Mankin, Carolyn. "Tales the German Texans Tell." *Singers and Story-tellers.* Ed. Mody C. Boatright. Publications of the Texas Folklore Society 30. Dallas: Southern Methodist University Press, 1961, pp. 260-65.

McGrath, Sister Paul. *Political Nativism in Texas 1825-1860.* Washington, D.C.: Catholic University of America, 1930.

McGuire, James Patrick. *Iwonski in Texas: Painter and Citizen.* San Antonio: San Antonio Museum Association, 1976.

———. "Views of Texas: German Artists on the Frontier in the Mid-Nineteenth Century." *German Culture in Texas: A Free Earth; Essays from the 1978 Southwest Symposium.* Ed. Glen E. Lich and Dona B. Reeves. Boston: Twayne, 1980, pp. 121-43.

McKay, Seth Shepard. *Texas Politics. 1906-1944: With Special Reference to German Counties.* Lubbock: Texas Tech Press, 1952.

Meusebach, John O. *Answer to Interrogatories in Case No. 396. . . . Mary C. Paschal et al., vs. Theodore Evans, District Court of McCulloch County, Texas, November term, 1893.* Austin: Von Boeckmann, 1894; rpt. Austin: Pemberton, 1964.

Moster, Thomas R. *A Diamond Jubilee History of the Sacred Heart Parish. 1889-1964. Muenster, Texas.* n.p., 1964.

Mueller, Esther L. "Log Cabins to Sunday Houses." *Diamond Bessie and the Shepherds.* Ed. Wilson M. Hudson. Publications of the Texas Folklore Society 36. Austin: Encino, 1972, pp. 51-60.

Müller, Friedrich. *Grosses deutsches Ortsbuch, vollständiges Gemeindelexikon. Enthält neben allen Städten und sonstigen Gemeinden die nicht selbständigen Wohnplätze der Bundesrepublik und der DDR.* 12., rev. and enl. ed. Wuppertal-Barmen, 1958. Of value for genealogical research.

Nagel, Charles. *A Boy's Civil War Story.* St. Louis: Eden, 1934.

Newcomb, W.W. *German Artist on the Texas Frontier: Friedrich Richard Petri.* Austin: University of Texas Press, 1978.

Nordhoff, Charles. *The Communistic Societies of the United States: From Personal Visit and Observation.* . . . 1875; rpt. New York: Schocken, 1965.

O'Connor, Richard. *The German-Americans, An Informal History.* Boston: Little, Brown, 1968.

Olmsted, Frederick Law. *A Journey through Texas, or, A Saddle-Trip on the Southwestern Frontier.* New York: Dix, Edwards, & Co., 1857; rpt. Austin: University of Texas Press, 1978.

Paul Wilhelm, Duke of Württemberg. *Travels in North America. 1822-1824.* Tr. E. Robert Nitske; ed. Savoie Lottinville. The American Exploration and Travel Series 63. Norman: University of Oklahoma Press, 1973.

Penniger, Robert. *Fredericksburg, Texas . . . The First Fifty Years.* Tr. Charles L. Wisseman. Fredericksburg: Fredericksburg Publishing Co., 1971. Translation of *Fest-Ausgabe zum 50-jährigen Jubiläum der Gründung der Stadt Friedrichsburg.* Fredericksburg: A. Hillman, 1896.

Pinckney, Pauline A. *Painting in Texas: The Nineteenth Century.* Austin: University of Texas Press, 1967.

Pochmann, Henry A. *Bibliography of German Culture in America to 1940.* Ed. Arthur R. Schultz. Madison: University of Wisconsin Press, 1953.

_____. *German Culture in America: Philosophical and Literary Influences. 1600-1900.* Madison: University of Wisconsin Press, 1957.

_____. *New England Transcendentalism and St. Louis Hegelianism.* Philadelphia: Carl Schurz Memorial Foundation, 1948.

Polk, Stella Gipson. *Mason and Mason County: A History.* Austin: Pemberton, 1966.

Quensell, Carl Wilhelm Adolph. *From Tyranny to Texas: A German Pioneer in Harris County.* San Antonio: Naylor, 1975.

Ragsdale, Crystal Sasse. "The German Woman in Frontier Texas." *German Culture in Texas: A Free Earth; Essays from 1978 Southwest Symposium.* Ed. Glen E. Lich and Dona B. Reeves. Boston: Twayne, 1980, pp. 144-56.

_____, ed. *The Golden Free Land: Reminiscences and Letters of Women on an American Frontier.* Austin: Landmark, 1976.

Ramsdell, Charles. *San Antonio: A Historical and Pictorial Guide.* Austin: University of Texas Press, 1959.

Ransleben, Guido E. *A Hundred Years of Comfort in Texas: A Centennial History.* San Antonio: Naylor, 1954; rev. and enl. ed., San Antonio: Naylor, 1974.

Raunick, Selma Metzenthin. "A Survey of German Literature in Texas." *Southwestern Historical Quarterly* 33 (1929): 134-59.

_____. "Was haben die deutschen Einwanderer und deren Nachkommen in Texas auf dem Gebiet der Dichtkunst geleistet?" Thesis, University of Texas at Austin, 1922.

_____, and Margaret Schade. *The Kothmanns of Texas. 1845-1931.* Austin: Von Boeckmann-Jones, 1931.

Ray, Worth S. *Austin Colony Pioneers, Including History of Bastrop, Fayette, Grimes, Montgomery, and Washington Counties, Texas.* Austin: Pemberton, 1970.

Reeves, Dona B., and Glen E. Lich. "Germans along the Guadalupe: An Approach to the Study of Cultural Diversity." *Die Unterrichtspraxis* 10 (1977): 33-39.

_____, eds. *Retrospect and Retrieval: The German Element in Review. Essays on Cultural Preservation.* Ann Arbor: University Microfilms International, 1978.

Regenbrecht, Adalbert. "The German Settlers of Millheim (Texas) before the Civil War." *Southwestern Historical Quarterly* 20 (1916): 28-34.

Reinhardt, Louis. "The Communistic Colony of Bettina." *Texas State Historical Association Quarterly* 3 (1899): 33-40.

Rippley, LaVern. *The German-Americans.* The Immigrant Heritage of America. Boston: Twayne, 1976.

_____. *Of German Ways.* Minneapolis: Dillon, 1970.

Robinson, Robert R., Jr. (Robinson-Zwahr, Robert). *Die Bremerverwandtschaft in Deutschland und in Texas* (The Bremers and Their Kin in Germany and in Texas). Vols. I and II. Wichita Falls: Nortex, 1977, 1979.

von Roeder, Flora L. *These Are the Generations: A Biography of the von Roeder Family and Its Role in Texas History.* Houston: Baylor College of Medicine, 1978.

Roemer, Ferdinand. *Texas, with Particular Reference to German Immigration and the Physical Appearance of the Country.* Tr. Oswald Mueller. San Antonio: Standard, 1935; rpt. Waco: Texian, 1967.

Romberg, Annie. *History of the Romberg Family.* Belton: Peter Hansborough Bell, 1960.

_____."A Texas Literary Society of Pioneer Days." *Southwestern Historical Quarterly* 52 (1948): 60-65.

Rosenberg, Amanda Fallier von. *Letters. 1849-1850.* Tr. Walter Wupperman. Travis County Room, Austin Public Library.

Rosenberg-Tomlinson, Alma von. *The Von Rosenberg Family of Texas.* Boerne: Toepperwein, 1949.

Rosenblum, Robert. *Modern Painting and the Northern Romantic Tradition: Friedrich to Rothko.* New York: Harper & Row, 1975.

Rutland, Willie B., ed. *Sursum! Elisabet Ney in Texas.* Austin: n.p., 1977.

Sansom, John William. *Battle of Nueces River in Kinney County, Texas, August 10th, 1862.* San Antonio: n.p., 1905.

Santleben, August. *A Texas Pioneer: Early Staging and Overland Freighting Days on the Frontiers of Texas and Mexico.* Ed. I.D. Affleck. New York: Neale, 1910; rpt. Waco: W.M. Morrison, 1967.

Sass, Hans-Martin. "Man and His Environment: Ernst Kapp's Pioneering Experience and His Philosophy of Technology and Environment." *German Culture in Texas: A Free Earth; Essays from the 1978 Southwest Symposium.* Ed. Glen E. Lich and Dona B. Reeves. Boston: Twayne, 1980, pp. 82-99.

Schmidt, Curt E. *Oma & Opa: German-Texas Pioneers.* New Braunfels: Folkways, 1975.

Schuchard, Ernst. *100th Anniversary Pioneer Flour Mills, 1851-1951: A Scrapbook of Pictures and Events in San Antonio during the Last 100 Years.* San Antonio: n.p., 1951.

Sealsfield, Charles. *The Cabin Book, or National Characteristics.* New York: St. John & Coffin, 1871.

_____. *Life in the New World, or Sketches of American Society.* New York: J. Winchester, 1842.

_____. *The Making of an American. An Adaptation of Memorable Tales by Charles Sealsfield.* Tr. Ulrich S. Carrington. Dallas: Southern Methodist University Press, 1974.

Seele, Hermann. *The Cypress and Other Writings of a German Pioneer in Texas.* Tr. Edward C. Breitenkamp. Austin: University of Texas Press, 1979.

Shook, Robert W. "The Battle of the Nueces, August 10, 1862." *Southwestern Historical Quarterly* 66 (1962): 31-42.

———. "German Migration to Texas 1830-1850: Causes and Consequences." *Texana* 10 (1972): 226-43.

Shuffler, R. Henderson. "Germans Who Went West." *American-German Review* 33 (1967): 10-13.

Shuford, Iris. *The Seven Timmermann Sisters: A Legend in Their Time.* Austin: Felix Shuford, 1976.

Siemering, A. "Die lateinische Ansiedlung in Texas: The Latin Settlement in Texas." Tr. C.W. Geue. *Texana* 5 (1967): 126-31.

———. "Texas, Her Past, Her Present, Her Future." Tr. from *Texas Vorwärts,* August 10-October 12, 1894. Dresel File in San Antonio Public Library and photocopy at the Institute of Texan Cultures.

Simonds, Frederic W. "Dr. Ferdinand von Roemer, the Father of the Geology of Texas: His Life and Work." *The American Geologist* 29 (1902): 131-40.

Smith, Henry Nash. *Virgin Land: The American West as Symbol and Myth.* Cambridge: Harvard University Press, 1950.

Smryl, Frank H. "Unionism in Texas, 1856-1861." *Southwestern Historical Quarterly* 68 (1964): 172-95.

Spell, Lota M. *Music in Texas.* Austin: n.p., 1936; rpt. New York: AMS, 1973.

Spiller, Robert E., ed. *Literary History of the U.S.* New York: Macmillan, 1948.

Steinfeldt, Cecilia. *San Antonio Was: Seen through a Magic Lantern. Views from the Slide Collection of Albert Steves Sr.* San Antonio: San Antonio Museum Association, 1978.

———, and Donald Lewis Stover. *Early Texas Furniture and Decorative Arts.* San Antonio: Trinity University Press, 1973.

Stephens, Robert W. *August Buchel: Texas Soldier of Fortune.* Dallas: n.p., 1970.

Stork, Rose Marie, and Oliver Stork. *Philip Peter Stork and His Descendants, 1798-1974.* Brenham: Hermann, n.d.

Stover, Donald L. *Tischlermeister Jahn.* San Antonio: San Antonio Museum Association, 1978.

Stumpp, Karl. *The German Russians.* New York: Atlantic Forum, 1967.

Taylor, Lonn, and David B. Warren. *Texas Furniture: The Cabinet-makers and Their Work. 1840-1880*. Austin: University of Texas Press, 1975.

Taylor, William Charles. *A History of Clay County*. Austin: Jenkins, 1972.

Tetzlaff, Otto W. "A Guide for German Immigrants." *Texas and Germany: Crosscurrents*. Ed. Joseph Wilson. *Rice University Studies* 63, no. 3 (1977): 13-19.

Toepperwein, Herman. *Rebel in Blue: A Novel of the Southwest Frontier. 1861-1864*. New York: Morrow, 1963.

Tolzmann, Don H. *German-Americana: A Bibliography*. Metuchen: Scarecrow, 1975.

Turner, Frederick Jackson. *The Frontier in American History*. New York: Holt, 1958.

Urbantke, Carl. *Texas Is the Place for Me: The Autobiography of a German Immigrant Youth: Carl Urbantke, Founder of Blinn College*. Tr. Ella Urbantke Fischer. Austin: Pemberton, 1970.

Walker, Mack. *Germany and the Emigration. 1816-1885*. Cambridge: Harvard University Press, 1964.

———. "The Old Homeland and the New." *German Culture in Texas: A Free Earth; Essays from the 1978 Southwest Symposium*. Ed. Glen E. Lich and Dona B. Reeves. Boston: Twayne, 1980, pp. 72-81.

Webb, Walter Prescott. *The Great Frontier*. Intro. by Arnold J. Toynbee. Austin: University of Texas Press, 1964.

———. *The Great Plains*. Boston: Ginn, 1931.

———, and H. Bailey Carroll, eds. *The Handbook of Texas*. 2 vols. Austin: Texas State Historical Association, 1952.

Weinert, Willie Mae. *An Authentic History of Guadalupe County*. Seguin: Enterprise, 1951.

Wellek, René. *Confrontations: Studies in the Intellectual and Literary Relations between Germany, England, and the United States during the Nineteenth Century*. Princeton: Princeton University Press, 1965.

Weyand, Leonie Rummel, and Houston Wade. *An Early History of Fayette County*. La Grange: Journal, 1936.

Wheeler, Kenneth W. *To Wear a City's Crown: The Beginning of Urban Growth in Texas. 1836-1865*. Cambridge: Harvard University Press, 1968.

Wiederaenders, Robert, and Walter Tillmanns. *The Synods of American Lutheranism*. St. Louis: Lutheran Historical Conference, 1968.

Wilk, Gerard. *Americans from Germany.* New York: German Information Center, 1976.

Williams, Marjorie L., ed. *Fayette County: Past and Present.* By the students of La Grange High School. Austin, 1976.

Willrich, Elise Kuckuck, and Georg Carl Willrich. *Letters. 1848-1850.* Tr. and ed. Minnie Groos Wilkins. San Antonio: n.p., 1952.

Willson, A. Leslie. "Another Planet: Texas in German Literature." *Texas and Germany: Crosscurrents.* Ed. Joseph Wilson. *Rice University Studies* 63, no. 3 (1977): 101-109.

———. "The Myth of Texas in Contemporary German Writing." *German Culture in Texas: A Free Earth; Essays from the 1978 Southwest Symposium.* Ed. Glen E. Lich and Dona B. Reeves. Boston: Twayne, 1980, pp. 241-55.

Wilson, Joseph. "The German Language in Texas." *Schatzkammer der deutschen Sprachlehre, Dichtung und Geschichte* 2 (1976): 43-49.

———, ed. *Texas and Germany: Crosscurrents. Rice University Studies* 63, no. 3 (1977). Wilson contributed an essay in this collection entitled "The German Language in Central Texas Today," pp. 47-58.

Wisseman, Charles L. *The Ludwig Ranzau Family.* Kerrville: n.p., 1972.

Wittke, Carl Frederick. *The Germans in America: A Student's Guide to Localized History.* New York: Teachers College Press, 1967.

———. *The German Language Press in America.* Lexington: University of Kentucky Press, 1957.

———. *Refugees of Revolution: The German Forty-Eighters in America.* Philadelphia: University of Pennsylvania Press, 1952.

√ Wooster, Ralph A. "Foreigners in the Principal Towns of Antebellum Texas." *Southwestern Historical Quarterly* 66 (1962): 208-20.

Wurzbach, Emil Friedrich. *Life and Memoirs of Emil Frederick Wurzbach to Which Is Appended Some Papers of John Meusebach.* Tr. Franz J. Dohmen. Yanaguana Society Publications 3. San Antonio: Yanaguana Society, 1937.

von Wrede, Friedrich W. *Sketches of Life in the United States of North America and Texas.* Comp. Emil Drescher; tr. Chester W. Geue. Waco: Texian, 1970.

Ziehe, Heinz C. *A Centennial Story of the Lutheran Church in Texas.* 2 vols. Seguin: South Texas Printing: 1951-54.

Zucker, Adolf E. *The Forty-Eighters: Political Refugees of the German Revolution of 1848.* New York: Columbia University Press, 1950.

N O T E S

Chapter 1

[1] Charles Sealsfield, *The Making of an American: An Adaptation of Memorable Tales by Charles Sealsfield,* tr. Ulrich S. Carrington (Dallas: Southern Methodist University Press, 1974), 27, 77, 117. See also A. Leslie Willson, "Another Planet: Texas in German Literature," *Texas and Germany: Crosscurrents,* ed. Joseph Wilson, *Rice University Studies* 63, no. 3 (1977): 101-103.

[2] Ottilie Fuchs Goeth, *Memoirs of a Texas Pioneer Grandmother (Was Grossmutter Erzählt: 1805-1915),* tr. Irma Goeth Guenther (Austin, 1969), 17.

[3] Ernst Kapp, "Letter, 1849," Kapp-Flach family papers, tr. Vera Flach.

[4] Friedrich W. von Wrede, *Sketches of Life in the United States of North America and Texas,* comp. Emil Drescher (Cassel, 1844); tr. Chester W. Geue (Waco: Texian, 1970), 96.

[5] Goeth, 15-16.

[6] Bettina von Arnim, quoted in Irene Marschall King, *John O. Meusebach: German Colonizer in Texas* (Austin: University of Texas Press, 1967), 27.

[7] Max Amadeus Paulus Krueger, *Second Fatherland: The Life and Fortunes of a German Immigrant,* ed. and intro. by Marilyn Sibley (College Station: Texas A&M University Press, 1976), 8.

[8] Ibid., 9.

[9] Goeth, 5.

[10] Carl Hilmar Guenther letter written at sea (1848), *Diary and Letters,* tr. Regina Beckmann Hurst (San Antonio: Clegg, 1952).

[11] King, John O. Meusebach letter of October 24, 1844, from Berlin to Count Castell, 32.

[12] Duden's *Bericht über eine Reise nach den westlichen Staaten Nordamerikas,* vol. 43, quoted in Rudolph L. Biesele, *The History of the German Settlements in Texas: 1831-1861* (Austin: Von Boeckmann, 1930), 3.

[13] Franz Kettner letter written on August 12, 1853, from Castell, Texas, "Letters of a German Pioneer in Texas," ed. and tr. Terry G. Jordan and Marlis Anderson Jordan, *Southwestern Historical Quarterly* 69 (1965): 463-72.

[14] Biesele, 69.

[15] *Der Auswanderer nach Texas. Ein handbuch and Rathgeber for Die, welche sich in Texas ansiedeln wollen, unter besonderer Berücksichtigung Derer, welche sich dem Mainzer oder Antwerpener Verein anver-*

trauen, Bremen, 1846, quoted in Otto W. Tetzlaff, "A Guide for German Immigrants," in Wilson, *Texas and Germany: Crosscurrents,* 14.

Chapter 2

[16] Caroline Ernst von Hinüber, "Life of German Pioneers in Early Texas," *Texas State Historical Association Quarterly* 2 (1899): 227.

[17] Louise Ernst Stöhr, "Die erste deutsche Frau in Texas," *Der deutsche Pionier* 16 (1884): 372-75, quoted in Crystal Sasse Ragsdale, *The Golden Free Land: The Reminiscences and Letters of Women on an American Frontier* (Austin: Landmark, 1976), 3.

[18] Friedrich Ernst letter written on February 1, 1832, from Mill Creek, Texas, quoted in G.G. Benjamin, *The Germans in Texas: A Study in Immigration* (1910; rpt. Austin: Jenkins, 1974), 17-19 in reprint.

[19] von Hinüber, 228.

[20] Ibid., 231.

[21] Rosa von Roeder Kleberg, "Some of My Early Experiences in Texas," *Texas State Historical Association Quarterly* 1 (1898): 231.

[22] Ragsdale, Auguste Ervendberg Wiegreffe interview in 1935, 41, 46.

[23] Ibid., Ida Kappel Kapp letter written on January 25, 1850, from Comaltown, Texas, 102, 107.

[24] Frederick Law Olmsted, *The Slave States before the Civil War,* ed. Harvey Wish (New York: Paragon, 1959), 131.

[25] Clara Feller quoted in Don H. Biggers, *German Pioneers in Texas* (Fredericksburg: Fredericksburg Publishing, 1925), 74.

[26] Ferdinand Roemer, *Texas: With Particular Reference to German Immigration and the Physical Appearance of the Country,* tr. Oswald Mueller (1935; rpt. Waco: Texian, 1967), 242-43, 272 in reprint.

[27] Ibid.

[28] Wilhelm Hermes, "To the Emigration Company Land on the Llano, Experiences of a German Immigrant in Texas," November 1846, quoted in Oscar Haas, *The History of New Braunfels and Comal County, 1844-1946* (Austin: Hart, 1968), 39.

[29] King, Peter Birk letter of January 15, 1850, from Fredericksburg, 135.

[30] Jordan and Jordan, Kettner letter of August 12, 1853, 464-67.

[31] Haas, Hermes quotation, 41.

[32] Prince Solms quoted in Louis Reinhardt, "The Communistic Colony of Bettina," *Texas State Historical Association Quarterly* 3 (1899): 33.

[33] This and subsequent quotations of Bettina are from Reinhardt, 33-40.

[34] Emma Murck Altgelt quoted in Henry B. Dielmann, "Emma Altgelt's Sketches of Life in Texas," *Southwestern Historical Quarterly* 63 (1960): 381-82.

[35] Looscan, Adele B. "Harris County, 1822-1845." *Southwestern Historical Quarterly 19,* no. 1 (July 1915): 52, 60-61.

[36] Goeth, 23.

[37] Hurst, Guenther letter of October 16, 1849.

[38] Ida Kappel Kapp, January 13, 1850. See also Sealsfield, 77.

Chapter 3

[39] von Wrede, 96.

[40] Dielmann, 373.

[41] George Bernard Erath quoted in Lucy A. Erath, "Memoirs of Major George Bernard Erath," *Southwestern Historical Quarterly* 26 (1922): 216.

[42] Henry Nash Smith, *Virgin Land: The American West as Symbol and Myth* (Cambridge: Harvard University Press, 1950), 170.

[43] Hurst, Guenther letter of February 6, 1853.

[44] Emma Murck Altgelt, *Beobachtungen und Erinnerungen,* manuscript tr. Guido Ernst Ransleben.

[45] Friedrich Kapp quoted in Lawrence S. Thompson and Frank X. Braun, "The Forty-Eighters in Politics," *The Forty-Eighters: Political Refugees of the German Revolution of 1848,* ed. Adolf E. Zucker (New York: Columbia University Press, 1950), 21.

[46] Friedrich Kapp quoted in Victor Wolfgang van Hagen, *The Germanic People in America* (Norman: University of Oklahoma Press, 1976), 92.

[47] Goeth, 40

[48] August Siemering, "Texas, Her Past, Her Present, Her Future," manuscript tr. from *Texas Vorwärts,* 1894.

[49] Goeth, 48.

[50] Joe B. Frantz, "Ethnicity and Politics in Texas," *German Culture in Texas: A Free Earth; Essays from the 1978 Southwest Symposium,* ed. Glen E. Lich and Dona B. Reeves (Boston: Twayne, 1980), 196.

[51] Ibid.

Chapter 4

[52] Caroline Louise Sacks von Roeder quoted in Dorothy Eckel Justmann, *German Colonists and Their Descendants in Houston Including Usener and Allied Families* (Wichita Falls, 1974), 36.

[53] Goeth, 32.

[54] Hurst, Guenther letter of January 1, 1857.

[55] Ragsdale, George Carl Willrich letter of April 1850 from Mt. Eliza (Fayette County), 61-62.

[56] Ibid., Louise Romberg Fuchs's *Erinnerungen* (1927), 70.

[57] Goeth, 41.

[58] Selma Metzenthin-Raunick, "Johannes Christlieb Nathanael Romberg: German Poet in Texas," *The American-German Review* 12, no. 3 (1946): 34.

[59] Ferdinand Lindheimer, *Neu-Braunfelser Zeitung* 3, no. 3 (December 8, 1854): 2

[60] Moritz Tiling, *History of the German Element in Texas from 1820-1850 and Historical Sketches of the German Texas Singers' League and Houston Turnverein from 1853-1913* (Houston: Reinand Sons, 1913), 136.

[61] Dielmann, 373

[62] Jordan and Jordan, Kettner letter of April 2, 1856, from Fredericksburg, 470-71.

[63] Earl Fornell, "The German Pioneers of Galveston Island," *American-German Review* 22, no. 3 (1956): 15-17.

Chapter 5

[64] Vera Flach, *A Yankee in German America: Texas Hill Country* (San Antonio: Naylor, 1973), 8.

[65] Francis E. Abernethy, *"Deutschtum* in Texas: A Look at Texas-German Folklore," *German Culture in Texas: A Free Earth; Essays from the 1978 Southwest Symposium,* ed. Glen E. Lich and Dona B. Reeves (Boston: Twayne, 1980), 206, 213.

[66] Krueger, 113.

[67] Ragsdale, Auguste Ervendberg Wiegreffe 1935 interview, 44.

[68] Hurst, Guenther letter of July 14, 1853.

[69] Flach, 6-7, 53.

[70] Kleberg, 297.

[71] Joseph Wilson, "The German Language in Texas," *Schatzkammer* 2 (Spring 1976): 44.

[72] Flach, 52.

[73] Ibid., 24.

[74] Ibid., 23.

[75] Ibid., 24.

[76] Mrs. Erno J. Bohnert in Comfort Historical Society. *Cooking in Comfort,* vol. I (Kansas City: Circulation Service, 1961), 50-51.

[77] Flach, 65.

ACKNOWLEDGMENTS

Preparations for this book have taken my family across Texas many times since 1975. Accompanied by my Scotch-Irish wife, whose regard for Germans is more detached than mine ever can be, as well as sometimes by our three small and unusually patient children, I have met friendly and interesting people who enriched this book by sharing their stories and experiences. I remember such visits with Leola Tiedt in La Grange, Mr. and Mrs. Leon Moser in Hurnville, Olga Rolater Whitley in Commerce, Major Anna Schelper in San Antonio, and Dr. Gilbert J. Jordan in Dallas. Similarly, Dr. Perry Donop in San Antonio, Joe Graham at the Institute of Texan Cultures, Marguerite Henry in Little Rock, Arkansas, and Sister Hubert Huber at the Subiaco Abbey of Benedictine Fathers in Arkansas patiently researched various topics for this book.

The book itself benefits from advice and guidance of five colleagues who have read all or parts of the basic manuscript. Foremost among these are Joseph Wilson of Rice University and Hubert P. Heinen of The University of Texas at Austin. Dona Reeves of Southwest Texas State University, Kent Keeth of Baylor University, and Mary El-Beheri's German class at MacArthur High School in San Antonio examined the manuscript with a view towards its effectiveness in the classroom.

I am greatly indebted to numerous earlier publications on the German Texans and to the host of local historians and genealogists who have preserved so much of the state's rich folklore and folklife. Chapter Two generally follows the chronology of Professor Rudolph Leopold Biesele in *The History of the German Settlements in Texas, 1831-1861*. To Terry G. Jordan I am grateful for his observations on the roles played by dominant personalities, on cluster migration, and on population origin and dispersal. A publication which was especially helpful to me is Crystal Sasse Ragsdale's exciting book on 19th century women's studies, *The Golden Free Land,* the title of which derives from the memoir of a dominant personality among German Texans whom we both regard highly. Without the kind permission also to quote extensively from Irma Goeth Guenther's translation of *Was Grossmutter Erzählt,* this would have been an incomplete study of the German people in Texas. Few of the early colonists were intellectual equals of the autodidact Ottilie Fuchs Goeth. A re-

219

cent work in a similar vein is *A Yankee in German America*, the reminiscences of Vera Flach, whose family graciously allowed me to extract material for this book. I further acknowledge the permission of Twayne Publishers of Boston to enlarge upon my own essay and to quote from those of Francis E. Abernethy and Joe B. Frantz in *German Culture in Texas: A Free Earth; Essays from the 1978 Southwest Symposium.*

Staff members of three immigrant ethnic museums in Texas shared photographs of artifacts, documents, and historic portraits: Margaret Bracher of Pioneer Museum in Fredericksburg, Linda Dietert of the Sophienburg Museum in New Braunfels, and Helen Faltin Martin and Paula Ingenhuett of the Comfort Museum.

Al Lowman of Stringtown, Texas, was a constant source of friendly advice and encouragement. My wife, Lera, and my typist, Carol Roane, assisted with the preparation of the basic text, the picture essays, and the features. Lera also worked with me to compile the "Chronology of Central European Colonization in Texas." My longtime personal debt extends to my parents, Mr. and Mrs. Ernst Perry Lich, of Cypress Creek; to our friends Mr. and Mrs. Guido Ernst Ransleben of Comfort; and to my paternal grandmother, Mrs. Tony Lich, née Hoerner. A *mater familias* from what is now nearly a bygone way of life, she started me reading German in *Fraktur* at the age of seven and encouraged me to begin recording what was, in fact, the social history of the relatively closed community in which I grew up. Her interest in the preservation of the past kindled my own.

Glen E. Lich
Cypress Creek
July 1978

About the Author

Glen E. Lich is a descendant of German immigrants from Hesse-Darmstadt, Nassau, Westphalia, Lower Saxony, Thuringia, Württemberg, and Switzerland who came to Texas and New Orleans in the 1840's and 1850's. Born in Fredericksburg and reared in nearby Comfort, he grew up familiar with the lore and folkways of the German Hill Country, where he lived until he entered Southwestern University at Georgetown in 1967. After advanced study at the University of Vienna, Austria, he entered the graduate school of The University of Texas at Austin to secure a master of arts degree in German literature and intellectual history. He later earned a master of arts degree in English and translation at Southwest Texas State University. He travels extensively in this country and in Europe, and publishes and lectures on folklife and literature of the Southwest, visual aspects of history, German-American cultural relations, and translation. He resides in the Hill Country.

221

PHOTO CREDITS

Page 2 Museum Folkwang, Essen, Germany.

Page 3 Private collection.

Page 4 Private collection.

Page 5 Historical Portrait Archives, Berlin, Germany.

Page 7 Isabella Braun, *Jugenblätter* (Stuttgart, Germany, 1861).

Page 8 Irene King, Waco.

Page 10 Museum Folkwang, Essen, Germany.

Page 11 Glen E. Lich, Comfort.

Page 12 Mr. and Mrs. Ernest Guenther, Austin.

Page 13 *Deutsche Literaturgeschichte.*

Page 15 Irene King, Waco.

Page 16 Mrs. J.R. Cade, San Antonio—Ottomar von Behr, *Guter Rath für Auswanderer nach den Vereinigten Staaten von Nordamerika . . .* (Leipzig, Germany: R. Friese, 1847).

Page 17 Rudolph Biesele, *The History of the German Settlements in Texas* (R.L. Biesele, 1964).

Page 19 Both from Sophienburg Museum, New Braunfels.

Page 20 Source unknown—Pioneer Memorial Museum, Fredericksburg—Source unknown.

Page 21 General Land Office, Austin—Source unknown.

Page 25 The University of Texas Barker Texas History Center, Austin.

Page 30 Texas State Library, Austin.

Page 31 Rosenburg Library, Galveston.

Page 32 DeWitt County Historical Museum, Cuero.

Page 34 Sophienburg Museum, New Braunfels.

Page 35 Irene King, Waco.

Page 36 Texas State Library, Austin.

Page 39 Prince Solms's Archives, Braunfels, Lahn, Germany.

Page 42 Sophienburg Museum, New Braunfels.

Page 43 Minnie P. Schladoer Collection, Mrs. E. Wayne Goff, Austin.

Page 44 Institute of Texan Cultures.

Page 45 J.G. Banik, Round Top.

Page 47 Olga Rolater Whitley, Commerce.

Page 48 E.I. Wiesmann, Keller.

Page 51 Source unknown.

Page 53 Source unknown; Texas State Library, Austin.

Page 55 The University of Texas Barker Texas History Center, Austin.

Page 61 Sophienburg Museum, New Braunfels—*Roadside Flowers of Texas,* Howard S. Irwin, paintings by Mary Motz Wills (Austin: University of Texas Press, 1961), page 27.

Page 62 Sophienburg Museum, New Braunfels.

Page 63 Institute of Texan Cultures.

Page 64 F.W. Simonds, "Dr. Ferdinand von Roemer, the Father of the Geology of Texas, His Life and Work," *The American Geologist* 29 (March 1902).

Page 65 Ferdinand von Roemer, *Kreidebildungen von Texas* (Bonn: Adolph Marcus, 1849).

Page 66 McNay Art Institute, San Antonio.

Page 67 Source unknown.

Page 68 Photo by Maryann Heimsath, Fayetteville.

Page 69 Glen E. Lich, Comfort—Kilman Studio, Fredericksburg.

Page 70 Institute of Texan Cultures—Bertha Grobe, Fredericksburg.

Page 71 Institute of Texan Cultures—Source unknown.

Page 72 All from the Institute of Texan Cultures.

Page 73 Institute of Texan Cultures.

Page 77 Helen Martin, Comfort—Gillespie County Historical Society, Fredericksburg.

Page 79 Harry Dietert Collection, Glen E. Lich, Comfort.

Page 81 *Harper's Weekly,* January 20, 1866, page 33.

Page 85 Archives Division, Texas State Library, Austin—San Antonio Conservation Society, San Antonio.

Page 87 Library of the Daughters of the Republic of Texas at the Alamo, San Antonio.

Page 88 Gebhardt Mexican Food Company, San Antonio.

Page 89 Major Anna Schelper Collection, Glen E. Lich, Comfort—Panhandle Plains Historical Museum, Canyon.

Page 90 Both from Lewis E. Daniell, *Personnel of the Texas State Government with Sketches of Representative Men of Texas* (San Antonio: Maverick Printing House, 1892).

Page 92 Pioneer Memorial Museum, Fredericksburg.

Page 93 Admiral Nimitz Center, Fredericksburg.

Page 94 Dwight D. Eisenhower Library, Abilene.

Page 95 Dudley G. Wooten, *A Comprehensive History of Texas* (Dallas: Wm. G. Scarff, 1898), vol. 1, page 597.

Page 96 Sophienburg Museum, New Braunfels—Olga Nagel, Fredericksburg—Major Anna Schelper, Kerr County.

Page 98 Sophienburg Museum, New Braunfels.

Page 99 E.E. Brodbeck, Austin.

Page 100 Lenz Collection, The University of Texas Barker Texas History Center, Austin.

Page 102 Adela Lich, Comfort.

Page 104 *Harper's Weekly,* June 15, 1878, page 481.

Page 105 Kilman Studio, Fredericksburg.

Page 106 Austin Public Library, Austin.

Page 108 Mr. and Mrs. Elwyn Paul Braunig, San Antonio.

Page 109 Both from the Estate of John F. Wilhelm, Menard.

Page 110 Barbara H. Green, Jacksonville—Institute of Texan Cultures, taken at the Lewis Tyne residence, Fredericksburg.

225

I N D E X

Page numbers in italic indicate illustrations or photographs.